University to Uni

University to Uni

The Politics of Higher Education in England
since 1944

Robert Stevens

POLITICO'S

For Robin and Rebecca

First published in Great Britain 2004 by
Politico's Publishing, an imprint of
Methuen Publishing Limited
215 Vauxhall Bridge Road
London SW1V 1EJ

10 9 8 7 6 5 4 3 2 1

A CIP catalogue record for this book is available from the British Library.

ISBN 1 84275 102 6

Printed and bound in Great Britain St Edmundsbury Press.

Contents

Preface

This book is designed to provide a background for the current debates on the shape, funding, educational and social purposes of higher education in England. The work is based on public lectures and seminars at the University of California-Berkeley, given in the spring of 2003. In turning these into more permanent form, I have kept the informal style of the public lecture, in the hope that what may be lost in academic rigour is compensated for by being more readable. While I have removed some of the comparative American material, I have left in much of the explanatory background material, in the hope that such material will make the sometimes turgid political history more accessible and provide a useful background for lay readers.

In developing these themes the intention had originally been to discuss solely the interaction of politics and higher education in the England of today. As I read and talked, however, I realised I had to reach back in time to understand the present. I also discovered, to my cost, that there is no convenient history of higher education – remarkable story that it is – for the second half of the twentieth century. The first part of the book thus became an attempt partially to fill that void. Its evolution reminds us that public and social policy in England is not made in great moves, based on some grand theory, but by jolts and starts as the result of political compromise.

One sometimes longs for the French obsession with theory and vision. As Lord Chancellor Irvine put it, however, in rejecting the 'purism' of the first Report of the House of Lords Committee on the Constitution in 2002, 'pragmatism based on principle, without the need for an all-embracing theory' was the English way. Perhaps, more honestly, one must say that higher education policy has developed out of 'muddling through', sometimes dignified with the appellation of the English 'genius for compromise'.

The first five chapters emerged from lectures and seminars given in the Center for the Study of Higher Education at Berkeley. At the Center, I am particularly indebted to Karl Pister, the Acting Director (and my successor as Chancellor at Santa Cruz) and the former Director, Michael Heymann, the former Chancellor of Berkeley. I am also grateful for the helpful insights of Martin Trow (who is in danger of giving up his lifelong study of British higher education, horrified as he is by the end of the binary line and the absence of academic input into the Dearing Report; perhaps he will relent after the Clarke White Paper)[1], Jonathan Douglass and Sheldon Rothblatt.

The last five chapters of the book are based on lectures, seminars and discussions on New Labour and the universities given at the Institute of Government Studies at Berkeley. These were a conscious effort to link the development of higher education policies to the politics of New Labour. Since the story finishes with the Clarke White Paper, it is inevitably unfinished business; but I can at least hope it pushes the debate forward. For this opportunity to put my thoughts on paper, I must thank the Director of the Institute, Bruce Cain, and

---

1.　See Sir Howard Newby's speech to the HEFCE conference, 17 April 2003, at www.EducationGuardian.co.uk.

his predecessor, Nelson Polsby, who now runs the British Studies Group at the Center, for this generous invitation. Nelson's insights on British politics are profound; his willingness to talk and read my material remarkable. I owe a debt of thanks, however, to all at the Institute for discussions both on higher education and British politics.

My social science-ey friends insist that a book which shamelessly makes so many value judgments must reveal at least something about my background and assumptions. I concur, reluctantly, since, while gregarious, I am an intensely private person. Nevertheless I am conscious that, having reached my eighth decade, I have lived through an educational revolution on both sides of the Atlantic.

Like so many of my generation, I was born to parents who, themselves born in Victoria's reign, had both left school by the time they were fourteen. My brother – my only sibling – stayed at school until he was fifteen.[2] I was lucky enough to go to a direct-grant school[3] and was the first member of my family to finish high school. At the

---

2.   In 1938. He then went to sea in the Merchant Navy on his sixteenth birthday, made a number of Atlantic crossings, was on a Murmansk Convoy and went down with his ship in July 1942, still aged eighteen. Today he would have been in his gap year. At eighteen, my father, in the fateful year 1916, was a trooper in the Hussars, helping the Irish to understand the benefits of British rule. He left Ireland to fight in Mesopotamia – eighteen months of persuading mules to drag caissons from Basra to Aleppo.

3.   Now, like so many direct-grant schools, a rather fancy independent public school. When I was Master of Pembroke College, the College had to raise rates for room and board in order to stay in business, and was faced with a rent strike. The *Daily Telegraph*, ever the protector of middle-class privilege ('How will the poor be able to afford Pembroke?') not only mangled my views on access and the reasons for the rise, but headlined that I had attended a £15,000 p.a. school! It is difficult not to concur with *Private Eye*'s custom of referring to English journalists as 'reptiles'.

4.   With the former Labour leader Neil Kinnock – or was it Senator Biden? – I cannot believe many of my forbears did not warrant a university education. My first cousin, Alan Fitch, left school at fifteen, found himself down the mines during the Second World War, eventually becoming a National Union of Mineworkers official, then Labour MP for Wigan, ending as Vice-Chamberlain of HM's Household (i.e. Deputy Chief Whip) in Harold Wilson's first administration. His son holds a PhD from the University of California, Berkeley.

time I was the first member of my family to attend university,[4] thanks first of all to a County Bursary and later, for graduate work, a State Scholarship[5] and later still a Graduate Fellowship from Yale. Growing up in England, I was thus a direct beneficiary both of the Direct Grant system and the 1944 Education Act, while, in the United States, I was the beneficiary of a well-endowed Ivy League institution. In turn my older children were beneficiaries of the California system of higher education based on the Master Plan: my older daughter studied at Gavelan Community College to become an FAA-qualified airline mechanic and my son at San José State, to become a registered nurse.[6] My younger daughter is at a private high school in England. Her chief contribution to the thinking behind this book was in 2000 when, aged twelve and already a listener to the news while dressing, she came downstairs, at the height of the Laura Spence affair, having listened to Labour ministers attack elitism in the old universities, to explain to me that 'I shan't be allowed to go to a good university, because I've been to a good school'.

Between secondary school and Laura Spence I had spent my life

---

5.   I attended Keble College, Oxford, then not a full college of the University, since it was not self-governing and applied a religious test. Its mission was to maintain the Catholic tradition of the Anglican Church and to take students from families without a university tradition. This latter was thought necessary because the reality of *Brideshead Revisited* still existed in parts of the University. The world has changed in the fifty-one years since I matriculated. The *Brideshead* tradition survives only in the minds of 'reptiles', Old Labour and bureaucrats in the Department of Education. Meanwhile, the barbarian hordes of evangelicals have desecrated the traditions and liturgy of *Ecclesiastica Anglicana*. It was also thanks to the generosity of the Gibbs family, another Tractarian family, that I became a Gibbs graduate scholar, which attracted a state scholarship, enabling me to have a fourth year to complete both my bar exams and a BCL.

6.   To complete the various levels of the Master Plan I should report my daughter-in-law majored in anthropology at the University of California, Santa Cruz.

7.   In addition to work on American legal history, I had written fairly widely on modern

as an academic and an administrator – mainly in the United States.[7] (When I graduated from university it was difficult to practise as a barrister without private means; British industry and commerce were only beginning to think about recruiting graduates and at that time English law faculties were not interested in my subject – modern legal history.) I would readily admit that my adult experience has been exclusively in elite institutions: an undergraduate and graduate student at Oxford, where I also taught for a year; then as a graduate student at Yale and a professor of law there for nearly twenty years. Later I was to be Provost (Chief Academic and Finance Officer) at Tulane University – an excellent regional university; then President of Haverford College – one of America's leading liberal arts colleges. At that point I was looking for a different kind of challenge and wanted experience of the public sector, as I feared that the elite private institutions were in danger of excluding bright students from poorer homes. (I was naïve: a well-endowed private institution with a social conscience is far more effective at attracting a wide socio-economic group of students than the inflexible public institution.) I turned down the Presidency of an AAU University (private) and was faced with the choice of either Vice-Chancellor of one of the Murray (often erroneously

---

English legal history and the English legal system and policies, since Yale was embarrassingly generous about sabbaticals, many of which I spent in England. See (with B. S. Yamey), *The Restrictive Practices Court: A Study of the Judicial Process and Economic Policy* (London, 1965); (with Brian Abel-Smith) *Lawyers and the Courts: A Sociological Study of the English Legal System* (London, 1967); (with Brian Abel-Smith) *In Search of Justice: Law, Society and the Legal System* (London, 1968); *Law and Politics: The House of Lords as a Judicial Body 1800–1976* (Chapel Hill, NC, 1978). On my return to England, I published *The Independence of the Judiciary: The View from the Lord Chancellor's Office* (Oxford, 1993); and, more recently, *The English Judges: Their Role in the Changing Constitution* (Oxford, 2002). In addition to contract and commercial law, much of my other work has been on the American Welfare State: e.g. *Statutory History of the United States: Income Security,* (New York, 1970); (with Rosemary Stevens) *Welfare Medicine in America: A Case Study of Medicaid* (New York, 1974; reissued, 2003).

called Robbins) 1960s universities in England or the Chancellorship of the University of California, Santa Cruz. With great sadness I turned down the English opportunity, but I was convinced (rightly) that the Joseph and Baker assaults on the universities (this was the mid to late 1980s) made the English offer part of a sinking ship. In addition to the better climate, California offered the chance of developing a liberal-arts campus of a well-funded university system, although that too shortly proved largely illusionary.[8]

By 1992 twenty years of teaching and nearly twenty years of attempting to run universities had left me with an understandable thirst for change. I decided to return to full-time legal practice and joined a Washington law firm. Long since an American citizen, I had assumed I had seen the last of England and of higher education. In fact I was asked to help develop my firm's London office, so I found myself back in England and, surprisingly soon, back in higher education. Approached to become Master of Pembroke College at Oxford, I found myself once more involved with universities and staying in England much longer than my proposed four-year stint in London. Inevitably, however, just as at Yale[9] and Haverford[10] I had found it intellectually important to think about the history and current status of higher education and the institu-

---

8. The money then dried up, though not as dramatically as in the UK. Nor did UCSC show much interest in developing a coherent liberal-arts curriculum, with a balance between teaching and research. It may well be that the effort to graft an Oxbridge in the Redwoods – with this balanced approach – on to the strongly research-orientated University of California system was doomed to failure. Today the failure is apparently accepted. In fairness, one should note that the balance is collapsing at Oxford and Cambridge.

9. See *Law School: Legal Education in America 1850-1980*, (North Carolina, 1983) and 'History of the Yale Law School: Provenance and Perspective' in (ed. A. Kronman) *Essays in the History of the Yale Law School* (New Haven, 2004).

10. *Philadelphia Friends and Higher Education: The Case of Haverford College* (Exton, PA, 1983).

tion I was involved with, so I found myself forced to think about where Oxford had come from and where it was going;[11] and what was happening to higher education as a whole. While I retired from the eminently civilized and enjoyable post of Master a couple of years ago, I have retained these interests in higher education in both England and North America.

One could say, therefore, that I have had a sheltered experience in elite institutions. Over the last few years, however, I have been seeking to understand the wider elements of higher education. I have travelled across much of England looking at a range of English higher education institutions. It has been an impressive experience. While there is considerable diversity in the new universities, the old polys play an absolutely vital role in linking Britain's industrial and commercial base with the older world of higher education. The staff I met were remarkably dedicated, sometimes operating in depressing buildings (something not unique to the newer universities) and, like all academics, inadequately paid. I was equally impressed by at least some of the colleges of further education. Some, like Tower Hamlets, not only struggle to bring into higher education highly diverse racial and social groups, but do it effectively. Others do it with less skill and commitment. Most suffer from the level of underfunding that the older universities have come to know only more recently.

At the newer universities, higher education and further education colleges, I should particularly like to thank Elizabeth Mytton, Chair of Post Compulsory Education in the School of Finance and Law at the University of Bournemouth; Sir Christopher Ball, Chancellor, and Dean Paul Bridges at the University of Derby; Dr

---

11. *Barbarians at the Gates: A View from Oxford's City Wall* (Lecture, George Washington University, 1998).

Geoffrey Copland, Vice-Chancellor, and his staff at the University of Westminster; Dr Annette Zera, Principal at Tower Hamlets College; Dr Roger Brown, Director, and his staff at the Southampton Institute. In addition, Nigel Savage, formerly Dean of Law at Nottingham Trent University and now a member of HEFCE, and Professor Claire Callender at South Bank University were most helpful on specific points. I also had the advantage of visiting the University of Gloucestershire and the University of the West of England.

While the newer universities were manfully (if one is still allowed to use that phrase) fulfilling primarily local demand (although for instance 5,000 of Derby's 22,000 students are foreign), the older universities were faced, not only with financial problems, but with the changed role of the liberal arts and sciences. Law, engineering, and medicine met obvious needs, as perhaps did chemistry, physics and biology, but what of French literature and Greek? Was there still a case for the training of minds? It was the so-called elite universities – not surprisingly since I had spent my life in such institutions – that fascinated me particularly. As both a UK and a US citizen I was particularly intrigued by the frequently inaccurate comparisons between the two systems – easily made since the diversity in American higher education means, as one commentator put it, 'the US, with 4,000 institutions of higher education, probably has fifty of the best universities in the world and undoubtedly has 500 of the worst'. I was also particularly interested in whether it was possible or desirable for Britain to maintain so-called international universities.

Some of these leading universities had been thought by foreigners to be – to use a trite phrase – among the best things the British had to offer. With New Labour's rebranding of Britain, particularly emphasised in the early months after May 1997, it seemed that these so-called elite universities (in the US they would more likely be known as 'centers of excellence') were to be designated along with the armed forces, the judiciary and the civil and foreign service as bastions of reaction. As it became less clear what would substitute for them as role models or elites in Cool Britannia, some elements of New Labour continued to attack them as socially divisive. While quality was increasingly accepted in research allocations, which critics might well have described as elitist, it was apparently unacceptable in teaching and other matters. Certainly the independence of academic institutions, at the heart of the best American universities, was frowned on. Centralisation, based on parliamentary sovereignty, is the basis of the English constitution, no matter which party is in power.

Thus much of the second part of this book inevitably attempts to unpack New Labour's approach to the enterprise economy, the meanings of elitism and excellence in current rhetoric and the clash between equality of opportunity (associated with New Labour) and equality of outcomes (associated with Old Labour). Much of this fight revolves around the word 'elite', which has a mystique of its own in modern Britain. In the past, the older universities from Edinburgh to Cambridge had no doubt they were producing elites which helped run the country. Their primary task was therefore to train minds and pass on cultural values. Today the word 'elite' has a particularly pejorative meaning. While the Council of the TUC, the editorial board of the *Guardian* and the Parliamentary Labour Party are elites, that is ignored; the judiciary, permanent secretaries and fellows of an Oxford college are seen as 'elites' and therefore bad. The fact that every society has elites, whether it is the Politburo in the old Soviet Union or the British Cabinet today, is quietly forgotten, yet it ought to be legitimate to question how those responsible for running the country are trained or educated, even if one wishes to avoid the French solution of the *Hautes Écoles*. Too often in England today the only question asked is how university education can help the economy. As part of this analysis the book chronicles the increasing insistence over time that the primary purpose of universities is not to transmit cultural values but to ensure the success of the economy. It also seeks to portray how far the role of universities, as independent actors in the political scene, has declined and concludes by asking whether that independence can be reinstated – assuming it is desirable – by the 2003 White Paper. In short, the book seeks to raise the basic issues facing higher education without attempting to articulate normative solutions.

For help with my efforts to grapple with these issues, as well as comprehending the funding of and planning for the whole of higher education, I am most grateful to anonymous civil servants in the Policy Unit at 10 Downing Street, the Treasury, the Department for Education and Skills, the QAA, and HEFCE. I can, however, thank Tony Clarke CB, former head of the Universities Section in the DfES, who, while he disagrees with virtually all of my interpretations, gave me insights which saved me from some serious errors. Dr Bahram Bekhradnia, formerly Head of the Policy Unit at HEFCE, provided perceptive background on the funding of universities. I have had the opportunity of meeting with the current Secretary of Education and Higher Education Minister in small groups. Their political advisers were also especially helpful. Sir Howard Newby, the Chief Executive of HEFCE and Barry Sheerman MP, Chair of the House of Commons Committee on Education allowed me to interview them. I have also had the opportunity of meeting with the spokespersons on higher education for the Conservatives and the Liberal Democrats. A wide range of politicians from all three parties has helped me understand their parties' approach to higher education and have read either the whole or parts of the manuscript. Once again, however, the interpretations of what has motivated different elements of the parties are mine and not theirs.

Having lived in Oxford I shall no doubt rightly be accused of writing from an Oxford viewpoint, although I have been a visiting member of the faculty at the London School of Economics and currently have an appointment at University College London. (And while I was a pupil at the Bar I also taught at a college now associated with the University of Wolverhampton.) I have also travelled around the older universities in the last two years, and talked extensively with staff at universities such as Cardiff, Kent and Southampton. I have also had the wise counsel of a clutch of vice-chancellors including David Eastwood, Vice-Chancellor of East Anglia, Sir Gareth Roberts FRS, formerly Vice-Chancellor of Sheffield (who also would want me to say that he disagrees with many of my interpretations), Professor Graham Zellick, Vice-Chancellor of the University of London and Lord Smith of Clifton, former Vice-Chancellor of the University of Ulster. The last two not only read the original manuscript carefully, but ensured that my grammar and punctuation met minimal – or is it minimum – standards. Auriol Stevens, former editor of the *Times Higher Education Supplement* and Professor Alison Wolf of the Institute of Education of the University of London read the lectures, and made insightful comments, helping me understand why things had really happened, especially at the sub-university level. Over the years, Martin Wolf of the *Financial Times* has helped me understand the principles underlying a more market-oriented approach. At Oxford, Harry Judge of Brasenose, David Palfreyman of New College, Dan Prentice of Pembroke, Peter Mirfield of Jesus, Ray

Rook of Pembroke, and Alan Ryan, Warden of New College, gave generous counsel. Kathie Booth Stevens, Clore Education Officer at the Ashmolean Museum, read the manuscript for style and sense. To all of them I am most grateful, but I must repeat I alone am responsible for errors, opinions and interpretations.

Finally I should like to thank Simon Blundell, Librarian of the Reform Club, who provided a research service comparable to the best American university. Gay Jenkins, Librarian at Covington & Burling, unearthed innumerable government documents. Pride of place in these final comments, however, should go to my secretary at Covington & Burling, Tracey Roberts. She decoded draft upon draft of illegible script with Zimbabwean guile and good humour. At times she effectively served as my research assistant. I should like to thank her and Lulu Parsons, who typed the final draft, for their efforts, and my law firm for allowing me to exploit them. Sean Magee has proved the most congenial of publishers.

I have dedicated the book to my younger daughter, currently incarcerated in an English boarding school, and my granddaughter, enjoying the delights of open air pre-school in Kauai in the Hawaiian Islands. May they both prosper at university.

Robert Stevens
Constitution Unit, UCL
15 September 2003

Abbreviations

AAU	Association of American Universities
AUT	Association of University Teachers
CAT	College of Advanced Technology
CNAA	Council for National Academic Awards
CVCP	Committee of Vice-Chancellors and Principals
DES	Department of Education and Science
DfE	Department for Education
DfEE	Department for Education and Employment
DfES	Department for Education and Skills
FE	Further Education
HEFC	Higher Education Funding Council
HEFCE	Higher Education Funding Council for England
LEA	Local Education Authority
LSE	London School of Economics
NATHFE	National Association of Teachers in Higher and Further Education
NUS	National Union of Students
NUT	National Union of Teachers
OECD	Organisation of Economic Co-operation and Development
OFFA	The Office for Fair Access
OUSU	Oxford Univesity Students Union
PCFC	Polytechnics and Colleges Funding Council
QAA	Quality Assurance Agency
RAE	Research Assessment Exercise
TUC	Trades Union Congress
UCAS	University and College Admissions Service
UCL	University College, London
UFC	Universities Funding Council
UGC	University Grants Committee

Part I

English Higher Education:
1944–1997

Prologue

The transformation of English[1] higher education between the Education Act of 1944 and the White Paper of 2003 has been a remarkable one. What had been a liberal-arts education for a small elite became mass higher education. It would be surprising if such a dramatic transformation had been accomplished with a full appreciation of the impact or indeed with any clear – or at least unchallenged – long-term vision. This first section looks at some of the fundamental issues, and attempts to explain what happened.

1.　The use of the terms 'British' and 'English' has become increasingly complex. For much of my life I have used the word 'British'. Indeed the word 'English' had faintly racist overtones, while the cross of St. George, the English flag, was seen only on country churches on the feast of St George. Perhaps it was the rise of Scottish and Welsh nationalism, perhaps the economic and political decline of Britain, perhaps the EU which allowed Europeans – and especially the perfidious French – free access to British shores, but the cross of St George is now prominent up to Hadrian's Wall and the Welsh marches. It flies from houses and pubs in a nation that – unlike the US – previously rarely flew flags. It now adorns the faces of young supporters at soccer, rugby and – God forbid – cricket games. Since devolution to Scotland and Wales (and the restoration of the Northern Ireland Parliament), England is now a legitimate political concept again. (Before it could only legitimately be used for the English legal system.) Moreover, beginning with the dramatic changes in the university structure in 1992, funding has been by individual country. Since 1998, Scottish universities are the exclusive responsibility of the Scottish Parliament, and the Welsh Assembly has oversight over the Welsh universities.

　　Another problem, also better faced at this stage, is nomenclature. I use 'tertiary sector' or 'higher education' to denote all of post-secondary education. Within the sector, too, it is possible for institutions to change status over a fifty-year period. So what was originally a technical college may become a technology college then a college of advanced technology and then a

In the sixty years concerned, the basis of higher education moved from training an elite to seeing higher education as a vital part of economic health, something available to as many as possible. Thus, a system that had been constitutionally entrenched – with twelve MPs representing the universities, whose graduates had two votes – until 1950, had, by 1997, come to be regarded by many as part of the public services. From being a privilege for the few, it had become the right of the many.

What was conceived of as a university had also changed. No longer was the vision of a university one which emphasized primarily the liberal arts – generally seen as the absorbing of cultural values which, while they might train the mind, served no immediate practical value except to produce an educated person and a potential leader. The primary purpose of the university was, by 1997, to produce graduates who would add to the economic success of the country. The old ideas were not entirely dead, but they were now in full retreat.

The most dramatic change, however, was in the sheer size of the sector. From having some 50,000 students in universities – or two per cent of the population – at the end of the Second World War, the tertiary sector was close to its goal of recruiting fifty per cent of the college-age population. In many respects this was a truly phenomenal achievement. Some, however, worried that, rather like the British Empire, the universities and other parts of the tertiary sec-

university. Or a technical college may become a poly and then a university; or it could become a college of higher education (offering mainly university courses) or a college of further education (normally offering both university and non-university courses, including A levels). This last fulfils the role of the old technical college of the 1950s.

What was, until 1944, the Board of Education (with a president) has also suffered transformation. It became the Ministry (with a minister) in 1944; the Department of Education and Science in 1964 (with a secretary). The title was shortened to Department for Education in 1992; expanded to Department for Education and Employment in 1997 and changed to Department for Education and Skills in 2001.

tor were 'acquired in a fit of absence of mind'. The first part of this book seeks, then, to outline the story from Rab Butler's Education Act of 1944 to the arrival of New Labour in 1997.

1. *The Emergence of English Higher Education*

Most institutions in England are covered in the mists of the Medieval, yet most are also basically the creation of Victorian reformers. Higher education falls neatly within that tradition. It operated, however, in an England which owed its style to a parallel political structure. The Act of Settlement of 1701, signalling the end of the Glorious Revolution, could have been implemented, as the Philadelphia Convention was to do, as a political system with the separation of powers, replete with checks and balances. As it developed, however, by the 1720s the Prime Ministerial system under Robert Walpole had produced a highly centralised form of what Lord Hailsham was to call in the 1980s 'elected dictatorship'. Yet as early as Thomas Gordon's *Letters of Cato*, in the 1720s, the inherently authoritarian and centralised nature of responsible government had been under attack.[1] To Thomas Jefferson the concept of having the King's ministers sitting in the House of Commons was evidence of tyranny and inevitably linked to corruption.[2]

---

1.   B. Bailyn, *The Ideological Origins of the American Revolution* (Cambridge, MA, 1992), ch. 2.

2.   Jefferson had no doubt that Hamilton admired the British system of government ('the most perfect government which ever existed') because it was based on the corruption of place-

The running of the country had, by then, been left to the Whig aristocracy – subject only to George III's attempts to regain control, leading to an unfortunate contretemps with the thirteen colonies. The Great Reform Act of 1832 symbolised the change. By the middle of the nineteenth century, the new liberal professional middle class had achieved supremacy in many walks of life, its arrival most firmly noted with the establishment of the modern civil service by the Northcote–Trevelyan Reforms in the 1850s. It was this class which put its intellectual seal of approval on the political solution of responsible government, permanently linked with parliamentary sovereignty by the publication of Dicey's *Law of the Constitution* in the 1880s. It was this linking that enshrined the top-down centralised basis of British government. This was the political setting in which the revival of the English university occurred.

It was one of the sons of the new intellectual middle class, John Ruskin, who observed that 'revivals are of things which never existed'. So it was with universities. Oxford and Cambridge had emerged in the twelfth and thirteenth centuries. By the Reformation they had become institutions producing what Thomas Cranmer, in his Bidding Prayer for the new Church of England, referred to as 'a supply of persons duly qualified to serve Thee in Church and State'. Those universities provided such a cadre until the Civil War in the seventeenth century, but in the more settled times of the Whig oligarchy in the eighteenth century, their purpose became predominantly social. Only in the Mathematics Tripos at Cambridge could it be said the English led Europe in intellectual terms. Yet, as higher education in the United States was reborn out of the excesses of Jacksonian Democracy after the Civil War, in England the tertiary sector of education reemerged in the middle of

men. Bernard Bailyn, *To Begin the World Anew* (New York, 2003), p. 50.

the nineteenth century out of a plethora of blue books – the new professional middle classes' secret weapon.

While there were certain inklings of reform at Oxford in the first half of the nineteenth century, it was the Reform Commission of 1850 which first began to force Oxford to look to the future rather than the past.[3] When Lord John Russell ultimately imposed the Royal Commission in 1850, the sloth in both teaching and research was castigated. With the exception of Francis Jeune, the Master of Pembroke, the University was opposed to all change, defending its clerical and collegiate soul in a report published by the university's governing body, the Hebdomadal Council. The Commission was anxious to make Oxford a centre of research and proposed a university dominated by scholarly and well-paid professors, with power ebbing from the heads of house, the colleges and private tutors. Needless to say, the colleges won and the Oxford University Act of 1854, drafted by William Gladstone, looked to reform of the colleges, to be conducted by them through an Executive Commission, rather than to reform of the university. The most radical step was to make it easier for dissenters to enter the university, although most colleges abolished restrictions on scholarships and fellowships and the new Hebdomadal Council began the process of weakening the position of Head of House. The rise of the power of the college fellows led ultimately to Parliament repealing the religious tests at Oxford in 1871.[4]

---

3.   On this see W. R. Ward, 'From the Tractarians to the Executive Commission, 1845–1854' in M. G. Brock and M. C. Curthoys, *A History of the University of Oxford*, Vol. VI (Oxford, 1997), p. 306; A. J. Engel, *From Clergyman to Don* (Oxford, 1983), pp. 33–43, 56–70. For parallel developments at Cambridge, see D. A. Winstanley, *Early Victorian Cambridge* (Cambridge, 1955), Peter Searby, *A History of the University of Cambridge*, Vol. III, 1750–1870 (Cambridge, 1997).

4.   The reforms of Oxford continued. As part of the colleges' redrafting of their statutes, some colleges had abolished – in whole or in part – restrictions on fellows' marrying. The 1877 Commission largely abandoned clerical requirements for heads of house and any religious tests

The world outside Oxford was, however, changing far more rapidly. In the 1830s Durham University – modelled on Oxford – had been founded, as had the University of London, composed then of University College London (UCL) and King's College, and of a far more radical disposition. This latter development was particularly important because UCL had no religious tests and was consciously open to all. The umbrella organisation, the University of London, was geared to providing external degrees, open to both men and women. This enabled Owens College in Manchester (founded 1850) and Mason College in Birmingham (founded 1875) to develop forerunners of those universities, designed as they were for local students and willing to teach subjects which included the vocational. In 1884, Manchester, Liverpool and Leeds combined to offer degrees of their own and in that same year Parliament began a modest grant to university colleges. By the First World War, the number of students at the so-called provincial universities exceeded the numbers at Oxford and Cambridge, while Birmingham, Bristol, Leeds, Liverpool, Manchester and Sheffield had all received charters as independent universities. There were, in addition, university colleges at Nottingham, Newcastle, Reading, Exeter and Southampton. In London, the London School of Economics (1895) emphasised the social sciences, ignored by the older universities.

---

for undergraduates. The battles between the researchers and the college men, however, continued. The former lost their battle to establish research professorships, although the rank of Reader was established. The reform of University government was politely passed over. The reality was that the professors and readers were to do research, the college fellows to teach by the tutorial method. It was one of those bizarre English compromises that was to last for a hundred years. Christopher Harvie, 'From the Cleveland Commission to the Statutes of 1882' in M. G. Brock and M. C. Cuthoys, *History of the University of Oxford*, Vol. VII (Oxford, 2000), p. 67. For the battles between the researchers and the college men, see V. H. H. Green, *The Commonwealth of Lincoln College, 1427–1977* (Oxford, 1979), especially ch. 16 and 17.

It was, however, in the same year as the Commission, 1877, that the first woman was allowed to sit her finals. The following year Lady Margaret Hall was founded, although Oxford did not admit women to degrees until 1920.

The nineteenth century also saw the reform of what was to become primary and secondary education. The provision of primary education, mainly through the churches, was becoming common by the 1830s, although not made compulsory nationally until Foster's Education Act of 1870. The century also saw the reform of the old educational charities, many dating back to the Reformation. Many of these restructurings of charitable schemes turned what were originally schools designed for 'poor scholars' into what were in effect private or independent schools for the rising – and increasingly prosperous – upper middle class, while they retained the name 'public schools'. The same movement, however, also saw a rise in local grammar schools – academic high schools – again normally based on local charities. Most of these were used by the middle classes, but scholarships provided an important means of allowing some bright working-class students to rise through the increasingly complex English class system with a chance for the best to attend university. A national system of secondary education to supplement the public (independent) and grammar schools was founded in 1902, while the invention of the direct-grant school allowed some independent schools to provide grammar school education in their locality.

Meanwhile the Technical Instruction Act of 1889 began the long and painful attempt by England to provide 'a good system of industrial education for the masters and managers of factories and workshops'. It had been a long uphill battle. Birkbeck College had started as the London Mechanics Institute in 1823 and by 1850 there were 600,000 members of the 622 mechanics' institutions. The movement largely failed because of the lack of education of the mechanics (compulsory primary education only arrived in 1870) and because the science relevant to industry and technology had not developed as a discipline. The institutes fell into the hands of the middle class, with artisans left to develop their skills through examinations provided by those remarkable Victorian institutions, the Royal Society of Arts (1856) and the City and Guilds of London Institute (1879). After the 1889 Act, local councils might levy a penny rate for technical education and the London County Council spent heavily on technical colleges. By the 1930s, in most parts of the country technical colleges were providing important support programmes for local industries and were beginning to supplement secondary education to provide rudimentary access to other parts of higher education.

By the First World War, therefore, England had two old universities, teaching traditional classical subjects, augmented by then with history, English and, almost as remote as the Sheffield Scientific School at Yale, scientific subjects. Most of their customers were affluent members of what we would now call the Establishment, living relatively expensively and luxuriously in residential colleges, but with some scholarship students from the grammar schools. For those emerging from the grammar schools the new civic universities were more accessible. They were largely non-residential, willing to invest heavily in science and engineering and catering primarily to the new Victorian middle class. Finally there was a growing technical education for the skilled and semi-skilled artisan, of varying quality and utility, but clearly separate from the academic secondary schools. These divides were to plague English education from that day to this, a problem only marginally ameliorated by the Workers' Education Association and other efforts at working-class further education.[5]

The First World War helped to focus the scientific needs of the nation. Modest grants from central government had become the

---

5.   R. C. K. Ensor, *England 1870–1914* (Oxford, 1936); K. Theodore Hopper, *The Mid-Victorian Generation 1846–1886* (Oxford, 1998).

norm. When the war ended, the Committee on Grants to University Colleges (1889) was transformed by a Treasury Minute in 1919 into the University Grants Committee. The Committee was responsible for advising the government on how much to give the universities as a whole and then deciding which universities should be given the money. It was a body with a majority of academics, who provided a buffer between the Treasury, which provided the money, and the recipient universities. The Board (Department) of Education was not involved because its civil servants were not thought of as being 'intellectuals' and might want to be directive. It was a cosy arrangement.

The inter-war years were not happy ones for Britain. Economic decline, social unrest and political stalemate were the order of the day. The Long Weekend, as social historians came to call the period, saw the creation of two new university colleges – Leicester and Hull – and Reading became a university. The forerunner of the Committee of Vice-Chancellors and Principals was founded, as were the forerunners of the Association of University Teachers and the National Union of Students. Overall, education remained depressed and the universities surprisingly irrelevant. School was only mandatory until fourteen and in 1938 only four per cent of seventeen-year-olds were still in school. The norm was for students, whether in public or grammar schools, to end their careers at sixteen or seventeen. University education was rare and arguably becoming less relevant, particularly as the civic (provincial) universities were alleged to be increasingly trying to ape the Oxbridge model. Technical education, while patchy, was undistinguished. It was in this atmosphere that it was perhaps surprising that Ernest Rutherford, in his laboratories at Cambridge, was inspired to split the atom, turning down a professorship at Yale because it involved teaching undergraduates.

2. *From the Education Act of 1944 to the Student Protests*

The Education Act of 1944 was for universities, as for other levels of education in Britain, a remarkable turning point. Secondary education became free; the school leaving age was raised to fifteen; and the basis was laid for the financial support of students (both through fees and maintenance) at universities. Yet if the clock were stopped in 1950, one would find a distinctly Victorian air about the tertiary sector. Less than two per cent of the college-age cohort went to universities. Physicians and surgeons, while they might have done a basic degree at university, often received their whole medical training at a London hospital school, which, while treated as part of the university sector, provided a purely professional experience. More than ninety per cent of solicitors had not attended university – except under a work release scheme. Their legal training was through an apprenticeship (articles); and the majority of barristers had either not been to university or had not read law at university; they had 'picked up' law at a crammers while preparing for the bar exams or later in pupilage (apprenticeship) in chambers. Nurses' training, at nursing schools run by the hospitals, included a varying amount of theoretical instruction but was predominantly on-the-job training; the bulk of the teaching profession was trained at a network of two-year teacher training colleges, frequently church-related. With a few exceptions, such as the Whitworth Scholarships, engineers were trained through apprenticeships, monitored by various levels of examinations run by the professional associations. Those planning to be pharmacists still did apprenticeships, supplemented by some work in the local technical colleges. Except for a handful of graduates recruited by the national papers, journalists learned on the job. The idea that travel agents or sports organisers needed a degree would have been unthinkable. Banks were not interested in recruiting graduates and industry was only beginning to do so.

What was remarkable during what was thought of as the most radical government that Britain had ever seen (Labour 1945–51) was just how irrelevant the tertiary sector seemed. As GIs raced back from the Second World War to take the benefits of the GI Bill at universities and colleges across America, the British Tommies returned to a society where tertiary education was virtually unknown, and, in any event, they would have been unlikely to consider it or be considered by it. The vast bulk of the country's secondary education – in so-called secondary modern schools – finished at fifteen and much of it was soul-destroying. If you had failed the intimidating 11-plus exam there was no second chance. Even for those at the grammar schools (the academic high schools) whether local or maintained or at the direct-grant or independent schools, education normally ended at sixteen with the taking of national exams – the School Certificate, still known generally as the School Leaving Certificate – the forerunner of today's GCSE.

Industry and much of commerce recruited their managerial class at sixteen or possibly eighteen. If any particular industry felt the need for testing, it could be provided by the City and Guilds. Each industry had its own system of apprenticeship ranging from the excellent to the appalling. Public-school (the powerful English private school) headmasters regarded with contempt New England's private preparatory schools, which prepared students for college and university. A good secondary education, culminating in the School Certificate or possibly the Higher School Certificate (the forerunner for today's A levels), was all a 'chap' needed to face the world. Going on to university was something one did if one wanted to be a higher civil servant, barrister, Anglican clergyman, consultant physician, or teacher in a public or a 'good' grammar school. Some country families still used Oxbridge as a finishing school, at least for boys. Universities were no place for women or, at least, ladies.

By 1954, there were some 82,000 students at English universities (and additionally 28,000 in teacher training colleges and 12,000 in full-time further education, that is taking post-eighteen education programmes mainly in local technical colleges).[1] Although only a fifth of university students were at Oxford or Cambridge, those two universities continued to dominate a society which was highly centralised and where the Civil Service was both all-powerful and Oxbridge educated. In the sciences, however, universities like Manchester and Sheffield were well funded and engaged in cutting-edge research. Even, however, at the height of the socialist revolution (the Chancellor of the Exchequer, Sir Stafford Cripps, opposed the UK's adherence to the European Convention on Human Rights because it was 'inconsistent with a planned econo-

---

1.   These colleges also taught an ever-increasing cohort of students doing non-higher education programmes, including part-time and sandwich students, taking everything from professional and craft programmes to sixth-form work.

my') the old elite system of higher education survived untouched. The University Grants Committee continued to decide what universities needed and the Treasury continued to honour the requests, allowing the UGC – dominated by academics – to determine which universities should get what.[2] The technical colleges, run by local education authorities (LEAs), had to rely on the generosity of the local councils, which in turn were dependent on the goodwill of rate payers. The universities retained their charmed and elitist lives. By 1950 students who had two passes in the Higher School Certificate normally had means-tested fees and maintenance provided at university, if they in fact gained a place, through scholarships awarded by the universities, state scholarships and county bursaries. The economic exclusion of the thirties was largely dead; although it survived among students in LEA-funded colleges and for part-time students.

---

2.   I have written elsewhere of the different US/UK approaches. *Barbarians at the Gates*, pp. 6–7: 'One of my favourite war stories springs from late in this era and neatly illustrates the difference between American and British cultures. In the 1960s, Yale was wrestling with its long-term future. In so many ways the Yale of the 1950s was like the Oxford of that era. When I was first an assistant professor, I remember the then president of Yale, A. Whitney Griswold, talking of Yale's solemn obligation to educate "a thousand Christian gentlemen" each year. There was an element of truth in it. When I began teaching there were no Jewish or Roman Catholic full professors in Yale College, and a strict quota on Jewish undergraduates. When, in the early '60s, Kingman Brewster became President, Yale rapidly transformed itself – ending discrimination against Jews, admitting women, beginning to take more students from public (in the American sense) schools than from preparatory (public in the English sense) schools, and ultimately seeking out minority students. Yale also began to take the sciences and graduate work more seriously. That, for Yale, was a remarkable change.

'It was in this context that Yale began seriously to consider its future funding. Griswold had seen the university as primarily the college with a limited number of graduate schools. Such an entity could survive on fees (paid by virtually all) and a significant, although at that time poorly invested, endowment. Brewster's vision of a modern research university, with its student body open to an aristocracy of talent, required funding. As alumni children were no longer automatically admitted, and fund raising appeared to suffer, the university first toyed with the idea of becoming dependent on federal funding. At that time – with John Kennedy in the White House and the *annus mirabilis* of Johnson – there appeared to be no end to the federal largesse. Brewster, who was no intellectual, was, however, concerned about integrity

Perhaps that made no real difference in a society that saw little or no role for the entrepreneur. The idea that universities should contribute to the economic success of Britain was not even thought of; and the intellectual wing of the Labour Party, while it might harbour hostility towards the public schools, remained largely loyal to the universities – and especially Oxbridge and London, where the non-trade unionist members had been educated. Yet the dominance of Oxbridge, while it may have protected the universities, had a high social price. As Edward Shils of the University of Chicago said of this period: 'If a young man, talking to an educated stranger, refers to his University, he is asked: Oxford or Cambridge? And if he says Aberystwyth or Nottingham, there is disappointment on the one side and embarrassment on the other. It has always been that way.'[3] It was not a system that could survive.

As the postwar bulge emerged from the universities, the demand for university places did not decline; indeed the reverse was true.

and independence – more so, I suspect, than the liberal faculty was. Yale eventually plumped for a world where Yale's independence would be protected by attempting to live roughly one-third from federal funding, one-third from student fees, and one-third from the endowment. Tenured appointments would be made only from the latter two-thirds, which was thought of as "hard money". If government money dried up, Yale would continue and no tenured faculty would be lost. The competing sources of income insured the independence and academic freedom of the university.

'I have used Yale as a base line because in the mid-'60s there were a series of seminars at Yale thinking about the future of higher education. At one, the British view was presented by Otto Kahn-Freund, then a professor at the London School of Economics, and by Tommy Balogh, the economics don at Balliol College, Oxford, then recently ennobled. They were horrified by the direction Yale was going in. The idea of raising money from alumni and corporations was distasteful, as were the charging of fees and a professorate whose salaries were related to distinction. They urged the Americans present to establish a University Grants' Committee (UGC). When the Americans asked "would not the piper ultimately call the tune," they were reassured by the visitors that it was inconceivable in England that the UGC would ever deny universities the money they needed or fail to ensure that the professoriate was comfortably paid. It was even more inconceivable that the UGC would ever tell the universities how many students they could teach or what they should study. Informally, the visitors opined that the inability of the United States to develop a mechanism to "sanitize" payments from government to universities was evidence of the inferiority of the American political system.'

3. E. Shils, 'The Intellectuals: Great Britain', *Encounter*, April 1955, pp. 11-12.

There were many causes although the most obvious was the availability of funding. Yet this change in fortunes was occurring at the same time – the early fifties – that the economic decline in Britain was increasingly apparent. The economic recovery which was emerging in the countries defeated in World War II – Germany and Japan – did not extend to the UK. The Suez fiasco of 1956 brought home to the British people the fact that the country no longer had an independent imperial future; it had to earn its own way. Finger pointing, looking for the culprits of Britain's demise, flourished. Management and the unions were declared defective; but so was the educational system. Public schools and grammar schools were under attack, but so were the universities and especially Oxbridge.[4]

The university world was, however, changing. The Butler Education Act of 1944 was beginning to bite. In 1938 only four per cent of seventeen-year-olds had been in full-time education; by 1962 it was fifteen per cent. In 1954, 4.3 per cent of the age group achieved university entrance qualifications and 3.2 per cent went to university. By 1961 the figures were 6.9 per cent and 4.1 per cent. The real pressure, however, was showing in teacher training colleges (where the numbers between 1954 and 1961 rose from 28,000 to 55,000) and full-time students in further education colleges (from 12,000 to 43,000, with a rise from 29,000 to 54,000 in part-time students.)[5]

With the number of students at universities having reached

---

4.   See, for example, Corelli Barnett, *The Audit of War* (London, 1986), blaming especially Newman's tradition of the primacy of useless liberal education as a prime reason for the economic decline of Britain: e.g. at p. 152; cf. W. D. Rubinstein, *Capitalism, Culture and Decline in Britain, 1750–1990* (London, 1993), especially ch. 3, which produces empirical data to rebut the Barnett thesis.

5.   By 1962, roughly ten per cent of all students were from overseas; women went on to universities at a far lower rate than men (2.5 per cent of the age group compared with 5.6 per cent).

113,000 by 1961, the pressure on the system was growing. The pressure was to lead to the creation of new universities, but to at least two committees which exemplified the polarisation of the university vision – such as it was – in the United Kingdom. The Anderson Committee, appointed in 1958, gave the last clear endorsement of the Newman view of the university, with the assumption that going to university was for the few.[6] Its Report was supported by the Hale Report on University Teaching Methods, published in 1964.[7] Already, however, the Robbins Commission[8] had reported. It had a much more imperialistic view of universities as well as a more inclusive view of higher education. Since Anderson had reported in 1960, it could be said that the transformation of English higher education was crucially changed in the years between 1960 and 1964.

To take the Hale Report first, that Committee was chaired by Sir Edward Hale, a Treasury mandarin, and former Secretary of the University Grants Committee. As Sir John Wolfenden, the then Chairman of the UGC, said in his introduction to the Report: 'the main object of an undergraduate course should be the development of the student's capacity to think for himself and to work on his own'.[9] The Anderson Report *Grants to Students* asked itself whether the government should pay all fees: no – it would be a

---

6.   *Grants to Students* (Cmnd. 1051, 1960).

7.   University Grants Committee, *University Teaching Methods* (1964).

8.   *Higher Education* (Cmnd. 2154, 1963).

9.   Hale at p. 3. The Committee itself was sceptical of the value of lectures and rejected the staff view 'that lectures are a good way of ensuring that the student knows what is required of him ... Surely the duty of the academic staff is to encourage students to learn for themselves and to seek knowledge for its own sake rather than to insist that certain material must be known for the purpose of passing examinations'. The engineering course at Sheffield University came in for special criticism, for failing to require students to think for themselves. *Ibid.*, p. 126.

waste of money.[10] On parental contributions generally the Committee was divided; it did, however, develop a more sophisticated method of means testing.[11] Those opposed to making entry to university easier by the state's picking up the tab put forward the challenging view that

> *university training was not the best lead-in to some of those positions in commerce and industry in which the nation must have brilliant but practical men and women... Nor is it necessarily the best preparation for a career in such socially valuable services as nursing, in primary and infant teaching, for which candidates of social ability and good secondary education are admirably fitted... It would be extremely unfortunate if there were any further growth of the opinion, for which there is even at the present too much support, that university education is a kind of national service to which all good students must aspire, and the possession of a university degree is an automatic passport, and indeed the only passport, to a position of affluence and importance, which it is the duty of the state to provide.[12]*

Abolition of parental contribution was also opposed by the universities, with arguments which some would regard as prophetic:

> *We oppose abolition for some reasons to do with universities themselves. Free provision of a much-prized good thing creates public*

---

10. Anderson Report, para. 153.

11. Those in favour of no parental contribution argued that the top tax rate was so high (then over ninety per cent) that it would be unfair; that the Australians had it right: 'brain power in the national interest must be encouraged'; and that there was no moral obligation on parents to support those over eighteen (paras. 167–76). Those opposed argued it would be inequitable while the independent and direct-grant schools had such advantages vis-à-vis Oxbridge; and 'self-reliance and self-respect are precious and not lightly to be exchanged for yet one more dip in the public purse'.

12. Anderson, para. 184.

concern about the methods by which certain individuals are chosen from amongst their fellows to enjoy the good thing. The controversy that has raged these last ten years in England and Wales over selection at 11+ for grammar school education is an example in point. We believe it would be bad for universities, and in the long run for the nation, if a similar wave of public uneasiness were to rise over selection at 18+. The danger we foresee is that, in the selection for university entrance, emphasis would increasingly have to be placed (as the number of applicants mounted) on examination marks only, claimed to be 'objective', to the exclusion of personal judgements of character and other relevant factors by assessors well qualified to make them. This could come about all too easily through public pressure on university authorities to provide a convincing explanation of the reason for rejection of every unsuccessful candidate. It would be against the national interest, in our view, if selection for university or equivalent education came to be based solely on the number of marks gained in public examinations.

The proposed change also involved other dangers to university independence:

If the parental contribution were to be abolished, the fees of virtually all university students (except those with their own private incomes and those from overseas) would be paid from public funds. Administratively, abolition would also tend, in our opinion inevitably, towards centralisation of payments. For instance, if all students from Great Britain were entitled to receive the full standard grant it might be argued that it would be administratively cumbersome for these sums to be paid individually to each student and that one small office working with mechanical aids should calculate and send to each university both the appropriate grant to

> *cover tuition fees for all its students and also the boarding fees for those of them living in college or halls of residence. We are not prepared to support an alteration that would seem so clearly to lead to a centralised bureaucratic control.*[13]

It was probably too late for the various concerns of the Anderson Committee to be taken seriously.

Already Sir Keith Murray, who became Chair of the UGC in 1953, was taking seriously an additional responsibility that the Treasury had added to the UGC's role in the late 1940s: 'to ensure that they [the universities] are fully adequate to national needs'. By 1963, Murray had created seven new universities – Sussex, York, Lancaster, Warwick, Essex, Kent and East Anglia – while cutting the formal links that held Newcastle and Dundee to Durham and St. Andrews. In the meantime the Robbins Committee on Higher Education had been appointed by Prime Minster Harold Macmillan in 1961 'to review the pattern of full-time higher education in Great Britain and in the light of national needs and resources to advise HMG on what principles its long-term development should be based'. The basic approach of the Committee was bullish: 'We take it as an axiom that courses of higher education should be available to all those who are qualified by ability and attainment to pursue this and wish to do so.'

The tone, then, was very different from the Hale Report. Universities were to expand indefinitely to meet need and were to be the controlling force in the whole of the higher education sector. Moreover, while admitting that the purposes of higher education were eclectic, the Robbins Committee put first 'instruction in skills suitable to play a part in the general division of labour...it

13.   Anderson Report, paras. 188 and 189.

must be recognised that in our own times, progress – and particularly the maintenance of a competitive position – depends to a much greater extent than ever before on skills demanding special training. A good general education, valuable though it may be, is frequently less than we need to solve many of our most primary problems'. It looked as if the economist Chair had put his mark on the future of higher education in England; the Newman vision was wilting. Robbins was prepared to offer some hope to a more intellectual approach: 'While emphasising that there is no betrayal of values when institutions of higher education teach what will be of some practical use, we must postulate that what is taught should be taught in such a way as to promote the general powers of the mind. The aim should be to produce not mere specialists but rather cultivated men and women.'[14] The camouflage could not hide the change of direction.

It is said that the Committee would have been called a Royal Commission but for the memories of Oxford dons about the nineteenth-century Royal Commissions. In truth, they need not have worried, although the dominance of Oxbridge was attacked. For the most part Robbins, while subtly changing its direction, reaffirmed the mechanics of English higher education, while emphasising the importance of skills and practicality. Teaching in small groups was favoured; universities were to be predominantly residential; students would be full time and should spend their vacations studying; degrees should be broader and the sciences should have joint billing with the liberal arts; there should be a balance between teaching and research; the nationwide uniformity of pay and standards for staff was assumed; maintenance grants for students should be the norm, although Robbins saw the time when loans

14.   Robbins Report, paras. 25 and 26.

would have to arrive.[15] It was, however, a bullish period. The Government White Paper of 1963 accepting Robbins announced: 'Courses of higher education should be available for all those who are qualified by ability and attainment to pursue this and who wish to do so.' Most remarkable in retrospect was the government's announcement: 'Plans are being put in hand and resources will be provided accordingly.'

In other areas the Robbins Report pushed the thinking on higher education into new fields. There was to be a move towards science and technology throughout the system. (The problem was there were never enough students wanting to study scientific subjects. Why this was so has never been fully explained, but presumably relates to the paucity of jobs and their lack of relative financial attractiveness.) There were already special institutions of scientific and technological education and research – Imperial College and the Colleges of Science and Technology at Manchester and Glasgow – with outstanding reputations. There were also to be new colleges of advanced technology – technological universities[16] brought under the umbrella of the UGC. Local and regional technical colleges – still under the aegis of LEAs – could give degree courses with degrees awarded under the umbrella of a Council for National Academic Awards. Teacher training colleges were to be linked to local universities and, for students who stayed for a fourth year, there could be degrees. The number in higher education in England and Wales was predicted to jump from 185,000 in 1962

---

15.   As a result of the Anderson Committee, standard systems of support replaced the old county scholarships and state scholarships, although both the maintenance payments and fees remained means-tested (i.e. students were supported on the basis of their parents' financial circumstances). At this point, however, the college fees at Oxford and Cambridge were not automatically included.

16.   Ultimately Aston, Bradford, Brunel, Salford, Bath, UWIST, Loughborough, City and Surrey.

(108,000 in universities, 49,000 in colleges of education and 30,000 HE students in FE colleges) to 481,000 in 1980 (291,000 in universities, 131,000 in colleges of education and 59,000 in FE colleges). Perhaps most interesting about Robbins were the matters that were not implemented: the links between Oxbridge and the state schools, the development of aptitude tests,[17] the establishment of seven new universities beyond the Murray universities, the support by generous grants of thirty per cent of graduates going on to postgraduate work, and the establishment of an independent body to determine pay for academic staff. These omissions were to dog the university system for the remainder of the century. Perhaps most intriguing was the Robbins recommendation, clearly made with the intention of protecting the UGC, as Parliament became increasingly interested in the costs of universities, of a Minister of Arts and Sciences, *inter alia*, to 'co ordinate' the UGC. The Conservative government (or, in the English way, the Head of the Civil Service, Sir Laurence Helsby) opted for the dissenting view in the Robbins Report by H. C. Shearman, Chair of the Education Committee of the London County Council, that the seamless web of education required a single responsible minister. As a sop for the 'High Church' view there was to be a separate Minister for Higher Education and Science and a separate Permanent Secretary. Basically, however, universities were henceforth under the Ministry of Education with its traditions of regulation and close contact with LEAs and the teaching unions. The Universities Branch now handled the UGC. Unlike the Treasury, the Ministry was thought not

---

17.   This is not quite fair. There was a university study done on aptitude tests. It found that an aptitude test was no better predictor than A levels – though O levels turned out to be a better prediction than A levels of class of degree (information from Alison Wolf). At the moment (2003) psychologists at Oxford are working on a new aptitude test, just as aptitude tests are being increasingly questioned in the US.

only to be unsympathetic to intellectuals, but, some argued, to excellence itself.

The atmosphere was not one of concern, however. Universities were the flavour of the month. They continued to be funded under the five-year block grants. The arrival of a new Labour government under Harold Wilson in 1964 seemed to add credence to the new university crusade, although, in fact, the Conservatives had already accepted the goals of expansion, at least down to 1967, and had committed the money. An expanded construction programme was pushed through the Treasury and five research councils were established. Wilson's enthusiasm for the 'white heat of technology' gave an impetus to the movement and the establishment of the University of the Air, which was the way the Open University was then described, only added to the momentum.

After a brief hiatus, Wilson (a former economics don at University College, Oxford), appointed Tony Crosland (a former economics don at Trinity College, Oxford) as Secretary of State for Education and Science. (He had previously offered the job to Roy Jenkins, who preferred to wait for one of the 'great offices of state'.)[18] Wilson and Crosland cordially disliked and distrusted one another. Crosland was a fascinating figure. The son of Plymouth Brethren, who believed neither in war nor alcohol and were trained to show no emotion, Tony Crosland saw active army service in World War II, drank prodigiously, and slept with a wide range of men and women until he married his second (American) wife. Crosland found the vice-chancellors, and particularly their lectures to him, a pain. He complained to his wife: 'I can understand about micro-economics. I can understand about sex. What I cannot

---

18.   He wanted one of 'the top 4 or 5 jobs'. Roy Jenkins, *Life at the Top* (London, 1991), pp. 170–1.

understand is the desire of human beings to hear their own voices. And, if one is to be truthful, I'm not frightfully interested in the universities.'[19] His intellectual, and in many ways moderate, social-ism was channelled into traditional Labour concerns. He appoint-ed yet another Public Schools Commission under Sir John Newsom. While it talked about integration and assisted places, the thrust of its Report was to do nothing. Critics of the schools prob-ably felt it was not worth doing much since the public schools were thought to be on the decline.[20] The direct-grant schools were exam-ined in the Donnison Report and their demise foreshadowed. The core of both the Labour and Conservative parties was committed to the comprehensive solution; Crosland was obsessed with it. 'If it's the last thing I do,' he pledged to his wife, 'I'm going to destroy every fucking grammar school in England. And Wales. And Northern Ireland.'[21] (In fact, he was not responsible for Northern Ireland.)

Crosland only began the process of destroying the grammar schools. More actually went under Edward Heath and his Education Secretary, Margaret Thatcher. Some LEAs never went comprehensive; there are grammar schools in Gloucestershire, Kent, Buckinghamshire and a few other counties to this day. In Northern Ireland they have flourished – both the Protestant and Catholic varieties – enabling English universities, which recruit vigorously there, to claim a higher percentage of state school stu-dents, for these grammar school students are extremely well

---

19.   Kevin Jefferys, *Anthony Crosland* (London, 1999), p. 109.

20.   While numbers of students in independent schools had risen slightly, the percentage of seventeen-year-olds in such schools was falling dramatically.

21.   Ben Pimlott, *Harold Wilson* (London 1992), p. 512. He saw nothing inconsistent in his wife's children, who lived with him, attending private schools

trained. This, of course, may change as Martin McGuinness, translated from IRA adjutant to Minister of Education in the province under the Good Friday Agreement, has announced plans to abolish them.

Thus, in an effort to rid the country of the dreaded 11-plus, and the tripartite grammar, secondary modern and largely undeveloped technical schools, Crosland and his Tory and Labour successors were responsible for the comprehensives, which, like the American high schools they were attempting to emulate, ranged from the relatively good to the perfectly appalling.[22] In place of the socially disruptive 11-plus, England had a system which avoided the sense of failure which characterised the old secondary modern. By the 1970s comprehensive schools at their best had serious sixth forms (and some LEAs had sixth-form colleges), making university entrance the norm; at their worst, some comprehensives had little sense of academic purpose or even educational purpose. Moreover, it was unfortunate that the development of comprehensives coincided with a move in educational circles to change teaching methods. The 'open classroom', 'mixed-ability teaching' and 'child-centred' education might have worked if they had been well funded. They were not. The new comprehensives were, in the eyes of many, doomed before they started. The grammar schools, which had taken bright and motivated members of the (mainly) lower middle and middle class and catapulted them (or at least some of them)

---

22. Labour adopted the principle of the comprehensive school after its defeat in 1951. Robin Pedley, the guru of the system, felt they would fail unless independent schools were forbidden from paying their teachers more than state school teachers (Robin Pedley, *The Comprehensive School*, Harmondsworth, 1963). Like American high schools, their quality tends to vary with the affluence of the area in which they are situated (and the concomitant willingness of the middle classes to use them). Thus in an affluent area like the Cotswolds there are academically highly successful comprehensives like Burford School, Chipping Norton School and the Cotswold School.

into the leading universities were – with few exceptions – dead. Oxford and Cambridge, which had done a remarkable job of democratising themselves since 1944 – by 1960 the majority of students were from state schools – found themselves with a decreasing supply of academically qualified students from the state sector.[23] Meanwhile the direct-grant schools found themselves sucked into the vortex of the loss of confidence in the grammar schools. The system had been established early in the century, with independent schools taking some state money in return for some state regulation. While nominally independent, they in fact provided grammar school education in the areas where they existed. Some now opted to join local comprehensive schemes, but the majority opted to return to their independent status, sometimes after failing to be accepted into local schemes.

The irony of the Crosland years was that his destruction of the grammar schools coincided with (and undoubtedly partially caused) a rapid increase in the numbers and prosperity of public schools and the willingness of parents to use them. While American middle-class parents were busily saving for college and university, as the result of the acceptance of the Anderson Report, all but the most affluent English parents had the fees (and real academic cost) of higher education paid and their children were provided with means-tested maintenance grants. Moreover all benefited from the significant government subsidies through block grants. Since English universities remained primarily the preserve of the middle class, the logical use of resources for this class was to spend heavily on private secondary education. Public schools, which had been

---

23.   Joseph H. Soares, *The Decline of Privilege: The Modernization of Oxford University* (Palo Alto, CA, 1999). Oxbridge was also much more successful than the Ivy League in producing scientists.

on the decline in the early sixties, were thriving again by the early seventies, augmented by the many former direct grant schools who had reverted to their independent status.

Before Tony Crosland left education in 1967 he was responsible for another important milestone in the history of English higher education. Already there was movement away from the recommendations of Robbins, which had seen the universities basically as running the whole of the higher-education sector. Colleges of education were to be linked with (in effect controlled by) the universities. Local and regional technical colleges might be considered for university status as things developed – which may well have been a euphemism for looking more like universities with a preference for full-time students. Indeed Robbins referred to a 'gratifying waiting list' of such institutions. While the Conservatives had accepted this aspect of Robbins, Labour was much less clear that putting technical colleges into an inferior position made sense. Eric Robinson of Enfield College of Technology,[24] an influential member of the Labour Party, fought vigorously for technical education, arguing that 'understanding the polytechnics is impossible without an acknowledgement of British class structures and class prejudice'.

Crosland himself was much influenced by Sir Toby Weaver, Deputy Secretary for Higher Education Policy – a former local government official – who persuaded him not to follow Robbins in these matters. Crosland began to talk about higher education 'for working people and their children'. He worried that, if incorporated into the

---

24.   Enfield Poly became the University of Middlesex in 1992. Eric Robinson ultimately became Director of the Lancashire Polytechnic (now the University of Central Lancashire). Robinson argued that 'there is a huge development of university courses which are designed with little or no concern for the students' future vocation'. Polys, he argued, should be teaching institutions: 'Students should come before research, before the demands of employers and before demands of the state!' Polys had a chance to 'change the pattern of higher education in this country.' John Pratt, *The Polytechnic Experiment 1965–1992* (Buckingham 1997), p. 109.

university system, there would be 'academic drift' in the technical colleges, and they would indeed come to look and behave like universities. The colleges of advanced technology (CATs), established in 1956, had certainly come to look like and ape the academic style of universities and were now under the UGC. As Crosland put it: 'For more than a century, colleges founded in the technical college traditions have gradually exchanged it for that of the universities. They have aspired to an increasing level of work, to a narrowing of student intake, to a rationalization of course structure and to a more academic course content.'[25] Much better, he thought, to differentiate the technical colleges from the existing universities.

From 1961 onwards, there had been increasing emphasis on technical colleges. The emphasis coincided with the growth in universities and the 'Golden Period' in the UGC. The question of how to look at the whole sector was settled by Crosland in his famous, or infamous, Woolwich speech on 27 April 1965, in which he said: 'On the one hand we have what has come to be called the autonomous sector, represented by the universities, in whose number, of course, I now include the colleges of advanced technology. On the other hand, we have the public sector, represented by the leading technical colleges and the colleges of education. The government accepts this dual system ...' While Crosland is later said to have regretted the binary divide, it was to shape English higher education until 1992 and beyond.

The new polys were to be under a separate funding agency. Responsibility for the establishment of the polytechnics fell to Roy Prentice, then a junior Education minister. He set out the goals in a 1976 White Paper: institutions which catered for full-time and part-time students, those on sandwich courses and those seeking

---

25.   John Pratt, *Ibid.*, ch. 2 and see especially at pp. 8, 10.

qualifications below university level. The suggestion was that fifty existing institutions be reorganised into twenty-eight polys (increased to thirty by 1973 and thirty-four by 1992).[26] The establishment of the polys also effectively ensured the demise of the plan to link colleges of education with universities. They drifted to the polys.[27]

The government had added a vitally important sector to higher education, whose goals were very different from the existing universities, which saw themselves as bastions of the learned professions, the liberal arts, cultural values and theoretical scientific research. Universities were to be unique. There was a more honourable reason for the change. By the sixties it had become increasingly clear that Britain's economic performance was falling badly behind that of other European nations. As Crosland put it, 'there is an ever increasing need and demand for vocational professional and industrial-based courses in higher education.' It was hoped that what became known as the polys would provide that technical expertise, in conjunction with the Industrial Training Act of 1964. The Industrial Training Boards were designed to prop up the declining system of apprenticeship in British industry. Few thought them a success. Such developments certainly did little to halt Britain's industrial decline.[28] It is unclear whether the idea that universities (and indeed the whole of higher education) were inex-

---

26.   DES, *A Plan for Polytechnics and other Colleges*, 1966. The assumption was that polys' uniqueness would be the part-time and non-degree programmes. It was thought to be a good place to expand because universities tended to eschew the relevant, were not easily controlled, and believed that 'more meant worse' (Pratt, *op. cit.*, p. 24).

27.   On this see Richard Layard, John King and Claus Moser, *The Impact of Robbins* (Harmondsworth, 1969), ch. 7 and 8.

28.   The average hourly increase in productivity in Britain between 1960 and 1973 was 4.1 per cent (compared with 6.6 per cent in France and 5.7 per cent in Germany). For the period 1973 to 1979 it had fallen to 1.0 per cent. During the sixties, Britain's GDP grew by an average of 2.4 per cent (Japan's was 9.3 per cent and Italy's 5.0 per cent). By the seventies the comparisons were even worse.

tricably linked with growth of the GDP came from government or the universities.[29] What is clear is that it launched an alleged relationship from that day to this and has been the catalyst for transforming the primary purpose of higher education from education to training. Equally, it helped transform higher education from a liberal education for an elite to mass higher education allegedly for the benefit of the economy.

The seven new universities recommended by Robbins had already been abandoned; but the UGC continued to request funds for the existing universities and CATs, which it expected to be met, and to make quinquennial awards. The economic climate made this increasingly unrealistic. Structural change was, however, in the wind. Soon after the arrival of Labour in 1964, the Second Permanent Secretary for Higher Education was abolished. In 1965 the Public Accounts Committee of the House of Commons gained access to the UGC and university accounts; and while in the early years the Comptroller and Auditor General was gentle with the universities, it was finally established that the piper could call the tune. As the UGC oversaw the doubling of the number of university students (between 1962 and 1972), the quinquennial grant called for a tripling in funding in a period of moderate inflation. At first all seemed well with the new quinquennial grant in 1967; the proposed recurrent grants for the next four years were generous.

The return of Labour in 1964 had, however, seen a run on the pound. Denis Healey, Roy Jenkins and Crosland urged devaluation on Harold Wilson. He refused even to discuss it. It eventually came in 1966, and Jenkins took over from James Callaghan as Chancellor

---

29. It was not unrelated to the emergence of the serious study of the economics of education, led by John Vaizey and Maurice Peston.

of the Exchequer. Jenkins managed to stave off a further devaluation in 1967 and the national finances gradually improved. It was not, however, a time when the universities, now predominantly funded by government, could expect to be left untouched. Parliament was increasingly asking questions about universities and especially the expense of new campuses. In July 1965, Callaghan, as Chancellor of the Exchequer, 'deferred' some of the building money; ultimately a fifth of the proposed construction for the quinquennium was lost. The National Incomes Commission looked at academics' pay (nationally there was then a so-called income policy) and were not generous[30] and even the increase was not implemented because of a pay freeze. Staff at universities increasingly unionised and government was more reluctant to fund pay awards. There was also disappointment that universities were not enrolling science students, an increase in whose numbers had been part of the rationale of the Robbins Report. Instead social science, sometimes in its more absurd forms, took pride of place.

Worse still – at least in terms of government support – was the arrival of the student revolt. Compared with Berkeley or the Sorbonne it was far more a protest than a revolution. (As S. J. Perelman remarked, the problem with England is that it is 'too couth'.) It could be argued, also, that whereas intellectuals and intellectualism were accepted in Paris and on the east and west coasts of the United States, they were frowned on in England. Whatever the reason, the more moderate outbursts in the UK were to have more lasting political effects than the student revolution, at least in the United States. In 1966 and 1967 student power appeared at the LSE and it spread to Essex and several other campuses,[31] not really sub-

30. National Incomes Commission, Report No. 3, *Remuneration of Academic Staff in Universities and Colleges of Advanced Technology* (Cmnd. 2317, March 1964).

siding until 1973. The net result was that the universities became a subject of hostility in middle England: in 1985 the *Sun* was still demanding the closure of the University of Essex.

By 1970-1 there were 236,000 students in universities (the independent sector) and 204,000 higher education students in the public sector, as the polytechnics were now called. The money to fund such growth, at least at the level to which universities had been accustomed, was just not there. Shirley Williams, the Higher Education Minister in the dying days of the Labour government, put thirteen points to the universities, all suggesting that excellence needed to be tempered by economy. The universities followed what was to become their normal procedure – they effectively did not respond.[32] Their attitude was understandably thought to reflect arrogance and complacency. Not only was higher education falling out of favour, but so was the Labour Party. In 1970 Wilson was replaced by the Conservative Edward Heath. The new Education Secretary was Margaret Thatcher.

---

31. Jack Straw, now Foreign Secretary, then a law student at Leeds and President of the NUS, acquired an MI5 file after visiting the future President Allende in Chile and being designated as a trouble maker by the British Ambassador in Santiago. 'Young Straw "a trouble-maker"', *Daily Telegraph*, 8 March 2003; 'Troublemaker in Chief: the future Foreign Secretary', *The Times*, 7 March 2003.

32. Maurice Kogan with David Kogan, *The Attack on Higher Education* (London, 1983), pp. 20–1.

3. *From the Student Protests to the Thatcher Prime Ministership*[1]

By 1970, then, the world was beginning to change. OPEC had begun to bite. Serious economic problems had become even clearer in the British economy. The student revolution had dampened the public's and politicians' interest and enthusiasm for universities.[2] Cuts in building programmes had occurred; could cuts in quinquennium grants be far behind?

The period between the Heath Conservative administration in 1970 and the Thatcher administration in 1979 represented the nadir of Britain's post-war history. The Head of the Civil Service, Sir William Armstrong, saw his role as 'managing decline'. On every economic scale Britain was falling behind both North America and the remainder of Europe. Edward Heath, himself, appeared as a believer in the market, but as industrial strife continued and indeed grew steadily

1.   The best survey of this period is John Carswell, *Government and the Universities in Britain 1960–1980* (Cambridge,1986). I have inevitably relied heavily on this volume. But see also Ted Tapper and Brian Salter, *Oxford, Cambridge and the Changing Idea of the University* (Buckingham, 1992); Nigel Allington and Nicholas O'Shaughnessy, *Light, Liberty and Learning: The Idea of a University Revisited* (Warlingham, 1992); and Peter Scott, *The Crisis of the University* (Beckenham, 1984).

2.   For confirmation of this, see Kenneth O. Morgan, *James Callaghan: A Life* (Oxford, 1997).

worse, he wobbled back to capitulation to the unions. One has the impression of his government casting around for answers; and finding none. In 1972, Heath, the only Prime Minister in the last fifty years to reject a serious Anglo-American relationship, took the UK into what was then the European Economic Community and is now the European Union (and, who knows, may shortly be the United States of Europe). To many it seemed the last throw of the dice.

Meanwhile the Conservative government sought to build on the 1969 Report of the Committee on Technical Courses and Examinations, attempting to strengthen vocational courses and apprenticeships to bring Britain into line with continental countries like Germany, which seemed to be able to link apprenticeships and universities and at the same time appeared unstoppable economically. Like so many things in the England of that day, the attempts went off half cock. The nationalisation – or at least centralisation – of apprenticeship had led to a decline in traditional apprenticeships and the establishment of vocational courses in further-education colleges (the colleges now below the polys in the hierarchy of higher education) of decidedly varying quality. (By 1970–1 there were some 100,000 students in FE colleges, far more than Robbins had predicted.) Nationally everything was going wrong. The oil crisis was a great blow. The government tried Labour's solution of an incomes policy, but the miners' strike and the three-day week saw the end of the Tories in 1974.

Margaret Thatcher, the new Secretary of Education, did not respond positively to the permanent officials in her Ministry. It was, she thought, an 'awful department'.[3] As she put it herself: 'The ethics of the DES was self-righteously socialist. For the most part, these were people who retained an almost reflex belief in the ability of cen-

---

3.   John Campbell, *Margaret Thatcher, Vol. 1 – The Grocer's Daughter* (London, 2000).

tral planners and social theorists to create a better world.' It was a department she found in thrall to the unions, especially the National Union of Teachers. 'Equality in education was not only the overriding good, irrespective of the practical effects of egalitarian policies in particular schools; it was a stepping stone to achieving equality in society, which was itself an unquestioned good.'[4] Mrs Thatcher tried to have Sir William Pile, the Permanent Secretary, fired. She failed. She tried to slow down the comprehensive movement in secondary education; she was largely unsuccessful. Whatever her sympathy for the Black Papers, then questioning the prevailing wisdom of the progressive educational establishment, there was little she could do. With respect to universities, however, the Heath government celebrated its arrival by downgrading the Minister of State for Higher Education to Parliamentary Under-Secretary.

Mrs Thatcher had 'no love for universities', although she did save the Open University. Her view of the universities reflected Malcolm Bradbury's *History Man*, the contemporary (and hugely funny) novel which implied that the new universities were repositories of mindless social science and social decadence, suffused with the ethos of the 'loony left'. Her contempt for sociology and the social sciences was considerable and after being physically attacked at Enfield College of Technology, her general view of students was not positive. As she wrote in her memoirs of the period:

The student protests of the time, far from being in the vanguard of progress, were phenomena of a world that was about to pass away. The universities had been expanded too quickly in the 1960s. In many cases standards had fallen and the traditional character of the universities had been lost. Moreover, this had occurred at a

---

4.   Margaret Thatcher, *The Path to Power* (London, 1995), p. 166.

time when market principles were in retreat and the assumption
was near-universal that everyone had a right to a job and the state
had the power to give it to them. So these rootless young people
lacked both the authority which had been imposed on their prede-
cessors in the 1950s and the discipline which the need to qualify for
a good job would place on students in the eighties.[5]

At the time, however, neither she nor the Department had the
relentless economic and practical view of higher education which
all parties eventually came to express. As the 1972 White Paper,
Education: A Framework for Expansion, put it: 'The government
consider higher education valuable for its contribution to the personal development of those who pursue it; at the same time they
value its continued expansion as an investment in the nation's
human talent in a time of rapid social change and technological
developments.'[6] All of these assumptions were questioned by the
disintegrating economic situation. For the universities this culmi-
nated with the decision of the Chancellor of the Exchequer,
Anthony Barber, in December 1973, to cut the incremental sum in
the remainder of the quinquennium by a half, which he cheerfully
announced 'could be accommodated without detriment to the
planned growth of the universities'. Shortly thereafter there was a
fifty per cent cut in the inflation payment for universities. The universities thus lost ten per cent of their budgets within a month.

The return of Labour, led by Harold Wilson, in 1974 meant
more of the same. Britain's economic decline continued. Labour
unrest continued; there was less money for everything. With less
money for universities – and more universities – the UGC increas-

---

5.   *Ibid,* p. 186

6   Cmnd. 5174, 1972.

ingly piped the government's tune.[7] It had warned in 1970 that 'it seems probable that the settlement for 1972-1977 will contain strong pressure to reduce unit costs'. Money for buildings evaporated and the expected expansion of students in the natural and physical sciences proved to be an expansion in the social sciences. This was increasingly frustrating to politicians and civil servants who had convinced themselves that more students in the sciences would ensure a higher GNP or GDP. The polytechnics continued to thrive, with their degrees (including by then graduate ones) validated by the Council for National Academic Awards. Increasingly their students were full time.[8] The universities changed little. They and the polytechnics, under the Crosland formula, continued to report to different offices; their trade associations were different; the funding agencies were not the same. Yet natural evolution operated. The polytechnics yearned to be free; they wanted a more research-oriented life and the right to give their own degrees; secretly some of them wanted to be like the old universities.

And still the numbers grew. When, under Mrs Thatcher's Secretaryship, universities were for the first time included in educational planning, the goal for higher education by 1981 was upped from 558,000 to 750,000.[9] Most of this increase was to be in the polys and the colleges of further education, as many of the remaining technical

---

7.   For a useful study of the declining influence of the UGC, see Michael Shattock, *The UGC and the Management of British Universities* (Buckingham, 1994), ch. 1.

8.   This of course varied from institution to institution. By 1992, 69 per cent of Plymouth's students were full time; at Nottingham Trent and West London it was 37 per cent. At Nottingham Trent 95 per cent of the registrations were undergraduates; at East London, the South Bank and Westminster, 15 per cent of the registrations were for taught masters. At Bournemouth, 37 per cent of students were on sandwich courses, while at City 18 per cent of the students were further education students. (Pratt, *op. cit.*, ch. 1).

9.   *Education, A Framework for Expansion* (December 1972). This White Paper made it clear that the bulk of expansion was to be in the polys. It also led to the development of higher-education colleges, a tier below the polys.

colleges had now become (thereby further confusing an already confused nomenclature). The notion of manpower planning and economic growth became part of the university planning rhetoric. It was this scene that greeted Reg Prentice in 1974, Wilson's Secretary of State for Education in his second administration. It was not an inspired choice. As the Senior Policy Adviser in No. 10 put it, Prentice 'seemed inactive'.[10] (He ultimately became a Conservative MP.)

While Labour was positive about education and especially higher education, the disintegrating state of the economy and the voters' alienation from the universities made help difficult. Universities experienced a ten per cent cut in students, and academic posts were frozen. Whatever fat that was left in the budgets had been squeezed out. While the Treasury ultimately put a little back into the pot, resources in the university sector were shrinking. The situation was not helped, at least in that sector, when the Houghton Committee recommended, and the government accepted, salary recommendations in the public sector (as the poly, technical colleges and education colleges were confusingly called) which in senior positions were higher than the national scale for university teachers. The AUT demanded at least parity, went to arbitration, and won, but then under a government freeze saw all wage claims limited to £312 per year. This left a gap in salaries between universities and the public sector. The public's loss of confidence in universities prevented the solution of the 'anomaly' for many years.[11]

There was more to follow. By 1974 the UGC admitted that the DES exercised 'strategic influence' on student numbers, while by

---

10.   Bernard Donoughue, *Prime Minister: The Conduct of Policy under Harold Wilson and James Callaghan* (London, 1987), p. 109. He added: 'Education policy was conducted by the local authorities and the teachers' unions with the Department of Education, as Harold Wilson once commented to me, being little more than a post box between the two.' (pp. 109–10).

11.   It is reported that in the protest by the AUT one academic carried the placard: 'Ameliorate the Anomaly'.

1976 it agreed the DES was responsible not only for student numbers but also the balance between arts and sciences and undergraduates and postgraduates.[12] In short, the government decided not only how many students there should be, but what general areas they should study. Meanwhile the cuts continued. The new government cut building programmes to their lowest level in twenty years. Building of subsidised student residences effectively ended. The UGC urged universities to buy fewer books. The government also raised the fees for overseas students and compensated by cutting the basic UGC grant, a process repeated almost every year. There was an important by-product of all this. As fees for both foreign and domestic students rose, since the government paid virtually all domestic fees, the UGC, with its funds cut by the amount of the increase, effectively lost its power to distinguish between universities as it distributed its funds. The government had discovered what was to become the 'unit of resource', decided by the government without the intervention of the UGC. By the time the quinquennium ended in 1977, funding was effectively on an annual basis and was effectively determined by student numbers.

Reg Prentice's successor was Fred Mulley (1975),[13] and he commissioned the first comprehensive study of the sector since Robbins. This so called Brown Paper,[14] finally published in 1978, was the work of Gordon Oakes, the Higher Education Minister. While it produced more honest figures (although still assuming that student numbers would decline with a dropping birth-rate) it was lacking in ideas, except for a proposed two-year degree for abler students (the

---

12. Shattock, *op. cit.*, pp 14-15.

13. 'Much more able than many realized but was not a leading member of the Cabinet.' (Donoughue, *op. cit.*, p. 109).

14. DES, *Higher Education into the 1990s* (HMSO, 1978).

Treasury preferred a two-year degree for the less able students because they could absorb less!). Already there were concerns that the universities were socially exclusive and links with economic success were increasingly mentioned. By this time the Education Secretary was Shirley Williams: bright, articulate and indecisive. The situation continued to drift. What was abundantly clear from the Brown Papers, however, was that it was the government's job to plan and fund higher education. Indeed, when an independent university was founded at Buckingham, inspired by the political scientist Max Beloff, politicians and civil servants were uniformly disapproving.

Other pressures appeared. As the Wilson government proposed devolution, both Scottish and Welsh politicians showed an interest in controlling 'their' universities. It was a warning of problems to come. There were, however, wider problems for the Labour government, led after 1976 by James Callaghan. In his famous Ruskin College speech, to the horror of the teaching unions and the Education Department, he asserted the need for more rigour and basic standards in the state schools.[15] Callaghan, who had not been to university, may have been the last Prime Minister greatly to care about them. To his Cabinet's horror, he even had a grudging belief in grammar schools. (He sent his own children, including the future Baroness Jay, to independent schools, as had the previous Labour Prime Ministers, Clement Attlee and Harold Wilson.) Callaghan's attentions, however, were elsewhere. Economic disasters forced Britain to be bailed out in his first year by the IMF,[16] while the political situation disintegrated still further. One of the recommendations of the IMF was that Britain should cease subsidising overseas students. It was a recommendation that Shirley

---

15. Morgan, *op. cit.*, pp. 502–3.

16. Morgan, *op. cit.*, ch. 3.

Williams accepted although, for reasons that are not entirely clear, the opprobrium fell on the incoming Conservative government, which had to implement her decision by ceasing to reimburse universities for the cost of teaching overseas students.

Before the government fell Williams had raised the fees for all students. To make her decision more politically palatable, however, she agreed to pay the whole fee for domestic students, irrespective of need. Included in this were the Oxbridge college fees, previously paid by parents or students, a decision which was to become a source of great bitterness in the 1990s. Only maintenance grants were still means tested. This remarkable gift to the affluent released funds to parents which increasingly were used to pay public-school fees. These schools, in turn, had become increasingly attractive as Shirley Williams did her best to finish off the last of the grammar schools. Meanwhile, the 'Winter of Discontent' (1978–9), rife with industrial strife, ensured the return of Mrs Thatcher, the relatively new Conservative leader, in 1979.

4. *The Thatcher Years 1979-1990*

By the end of the seventies then, along with the remainder of Britain, the universities were suffering from loss of public confidence. This was caused by the student revolution; the growth in numbers which inevitably led to increasing interest in what were, by then, the massive funds going into the tertiary sector; and the distressed state of the British economy. Yet visitors in the late seventies still talked of the leading British universities as on a par with the leading American universities and European commentators rated English universities as the best in Europe. It was a situation which was to change rapidly.

Mrs Thatcher is renowned in the United States as the guru of freedom and the market, privatisation and the curbing of the unions. While she did vitally shake up the British economy, she nevertheless despised universities. She, partly deliberately, and possibly partly unconsciously, set out to undermine them. She (or her administration) curbed the independence of universities dramatically and set up a system of central control worthy of India, Cuba, Russia or China at their most extreme stage of central planning.[1] Some planning was the inevitable concomitant of govern-

---

1.   The best description of this is chapter 7 of Simon Jenkins's *Accountable to None: The Tory Nationalisation of Britain* (London, 1995).

ment as paymaster; the Conservatives increasingly insisted on total control. Already, as we saw, the quinquennial grant had been abandoned by 1974 and as early as 1968 the UGC had conceded the need 'for at least the outline of a central strategy'. In addition to the protection of independence provided by the UGC, the notional survival of fees gave a further boost, in effect providing a student with a voucher to use at the university of his or her choice. During the seventies the Treasury had refused to increase the size of university fees, paid through the local authorities, in line with inflation, because it meant simply that the Treasury had to increase the budgets of local authorities. (This was especially true after Shirley Williams had abandoned the parental contribution.) That decision, however, meant that universities were ever more dependent on central funds. With the UGC now working on yearly budgets, the new government decided to halve fees, quite deliberately because they wanted to control universities more effectively.

Since the universities were now effectively totally dependent on government for funding, the most obvious way to do this was by fiscal constraint. The new Secretary of State for Education was Mark Carlisle, whose period at the Ministry – as it then was – was marked chiefly by reports of his returning 'bleeding' from encounters with the Treasury. By 1981, he had been replaced by Sir Keith Joseph, a prophet of the free market (indeed many thought he inspired Mrs Thatcher's embracing of the market). Joseph believed in cutting government spending and lowering taxes. He made little effort to stop the Treasury reducing his departmental budget. By the time Carlisle had discussed university spending for 1980-81, the Treasury looked for an eight per cent cut compared with 1979. The following years were to have cuts of five per cent in real terms.[2] In

---

2.   On this period see Kogan and Kogan, *op. cit.*, ch. 4 *et seq.*

1981 the universities were given a month to make an eighteen per cent cut in their budgets.[3] Three thousand academic posts were eliminated.

The UGC rather ineffectively tried to become a planning agency, with efforts to quantify the research productivity of departments.[4] As Sir Edward Parkes, the Chairman of the UGC, warned, however, 'the greatest threat to the United Kingdom universities today is not a financial one'. It was not just that Sir Keith Joseph was cutting the grants for the then new universities – Bradford, Salford and Aston – by thirty per cent; he was suggesting the end of tenure. (Tenure in England, however, was closer to a presumption of continuous employment than the American version of tenure.) Moreover it was increasingly obvious that the government was unhappy with a UGC that had such a 'cosy' relationship with universities. The UGC, as it managed decline, was increasingly required to be the government's agent.

Keith Joseph[5] is an interesting figure. Highly intelligent and not very worldly, he was dubbed 'The Mad Monk' by the satirical magazine *Private Eye*. He was not a particularly effective lobbyist in the spending rounds in which ministers must argue their department's cases with the Treasury (which performs the role historically taken by the Office of Management and Budget in the USA). Perhaps it was that Joseph had little sympathy with much that had happened. He thought the expansion of higher education had gone too far and that students and universities had lost their way. At one point he even invited the Treasury to make further cuts. He wanted fewer

---

3. The hardest hit was Salford, which saw its budget cut 40 per cent in three years.

4. Shattock argues that the UGC regained the initiative between 1978 and 1983, *op. cit.*, p. 20 *et seq.*

5. Andrew Denham and Mark Garnett, *Keith Joseph* (Chesham, 2001).

students (there was still an incorrect assumption that as the number of eighteen-year-olds dropped, student numbers would drop) and, in any event, more of them in polytechnics rather than universities. At the secondary level he was opposed to comprehensives and developed the Assisted Places Scheme – to bring bright students from the state schools to the private schools. He also toyed with vouchers for parents choosing secondary education.

The students were outraged by the cuts in numbers and Joseph was physically attacked in Brighton. Academics, too, accustomed to block grant funding, could not adjust to the loss of public esteem and ring-fenced funding. Not only did they continue their somewhat pretentious habit of signing petitions about political situations in all parts of the world, they increasingly started attacking the government. Some 364 economists attacked Geoffrey Howe's budget, a budget by which the Chancellor of the Exchequer began the process of moving Britain away from the planned economy[6] (of course with the exception of the universities). Even before that, however, the academics had been outraged by the 1979 decision – blamed on the Conservatives – to charge economic fees to overseas students, the receipt of which the Treasury compensated for by reducing university grants. In the end the universities capitulated and higher fees came in.[7] The anger about the increases and the cuts remained. After the return of the Conservatives, basking in 'the Falklands effect' in 1983, Oxford's Hebdomadal

---

6.   Geoffrey Howe, *Conflict of Loyalty* (London, 1994), *passim*.

7.   At Oxford, Congregation, the meeting of dons, ordered colleges, which had separate fees, not to increase fees to overseas students. The richer colleges could afford this; the decision worsened still further the financial condition of the poorer colleges. The right of Oxford dons to have the final say on all matters in Congregation has done considerable damage to the university over the years. Not only were there votes against overseas fees, but there was also the Thatcher honorary degree. The Wafic Said gift was also thrown into doubt. It is all rather reminiscent of Bill Buckley's observation that he would rather be governed by the first 500 names in the Boston telephone directory than the faculty of Harvard College. He is of course a Yale man. But see William F. Buckley Jr., *God and Man at Yale* (Chicago, 1951), *passim*.

Council decided to award Mrs Thatcher, an Oxford graduate, an honorary degree. Oxford had always awarded an honorary DCL to Oxonian Prime Ministers. Congregation, the legislature of Oxford academics, publicly rejected it. No doubt the dons felt better, but they lost the public-relations battle.[8] While Halsey[9] reported the gradual move in the political views of academics towards the left, the British public showed greater faith in Mrs Thatcher.

The year 1984 was indeed the year of Big Brother, at least in the eyes of many academics. Pressure from the DES (Department of Education and Science) had already seen efforts to merge or eliminate weak university departments coupled with money for early retirement to reduce the number of academics. In 1984, under pressure from the DES, the UGC announced that 'to ensure that resources for research are allocated and managed to their best advantage' they would be allocated selectively, rather than distributed primarily through the block grant in an egalitarian way (pro rata according to the number of students) to the then existing universities. No longer would the universities and the UGC be the primary determinants of research. The Advisory Board for Research Councils – allocating research grants in addition to the block grants and under the aegis of the Department of Trade and Industry – became far more proactive.[10] While some

---

8.   The best accounts of this are Anthony Kenny, *A Life in Oxford* (London, 1997), ch. 17 ('Oxford v Thatcher'); Hugo Young, *One of Us: A Biography of Margaret Thatcher* (London, 1989), pp. 401–3. The vote was 738–319. A total of 275 dons signed the petition, alleging Mrs Thatcher had 'done deep and systematic damage to the whole public education system in Britain'. Mrs Thatcher responded: 'If they do not wish to confer the honour, I am the last person who would wish to receive it.' For a sense of the academics' reaction to the Thatcher years, see Noel Annan, *The Dons: Mentors, Eccentrics and Geniuses* (London, 1999), especially ch. 14.

9.   A. H. Halsey, *The Decline of Donnish Dominion: The British Academic Profession in the Twentieth Century* (Oxford, 1992), ch. 11.

10.   See Shattock, *op. cit.*, ch. 2. The emphasis on excellence was primarily attributed to William Waldegrave, Higher Education Minister 1981–3.

leading scientists at the major universities protested, the move in
fact protected research in these universities as the country moved
to a more egalitarian general funding base for the bulk of universities.

By 1984, academics, picking up the Conservatives' interest –
amounting almost to an obsession – with the link between university research and graduates on the one hand and economic growth
on the other, argued that the ongoing cuts in university funding
were harming industry. As early as 1982, William Waldegrave, then
the Higher Education Minister, had argued that 'government,
industry and higher education must work together to match the
output of qualified personnel with industry's needs'.[11] Keith
Joseph, kept on after the 1983 election more because of his loyalty
to Margaret Thatcher than because of his competence as a minister, thought he saw a way of closing the fiscal gap, and pushing far
more money towards science. On 12 November 1984, Joseph
announced that the university maintenance grant would have lower
thresholds for means testing, meaning the affluent would pay more.
More terrifying to Middle England, he announced a £725 to
£4,000 university fee, means-tested, to be paid by richer parents.
Moreover, the increases were to become effective at once.
Conservative backbenchers, prodded by Tory voters, were outraged. Joseph was denounced as 'a secret socialist' and 180 Tory
MPs signed a hostile motion.[12] On 4 December, 250 Tory MPs met
in Committee Room 14 and Joseph was subjected to a vicious ver-
bal attack by the irate mob of table-pounding Tory backbenchers

---

11.   Pratt, *op. cit.*, p. 22.

12.   As a letter in *The Times* put it: 'Life insurance premium relief abolished, VAT imposed
on home building improvement, and now extensive charges for higher education, all aimed
squarely at those who hold to the principles of self help and family betterment.' Cited by Peter
Jenkins, *Mrs. Thatcher's Revolution: The Ending of a Socialist Era* (Harvard, 1988), p. 182.

who, in the words of Nigel Lawson, believed 'Keith had no political judgement'. The following day Mrs Thatcher withdrew her
support for the proposal, claiming that she had not been properly
briefed;[13] and Keith Joseph cut the funding of science research to
fill the financial gap.

Some Conservative backbenchers, of course, had more intellectual concerns. Enoch Powell observed: 'It is barbarism to attempt to
evaluate the contents of higher education in terms of economic performance, or to set a value upon the consequences of higher education in terms of monetary cost-benefit analysis.' Powell had been a
professor of Greek. Robert Rhodes James MP, a former Cambridge
don, put it differently: the DES 'had no understanding of the purpose of a university'. George Walden, who was Parliamentary
Private Secretary and then Parliamentary Under Secretary in the
DES from 1983 to 1987, with responsibility for higher education,
has recorded the mood during these years. Walden, an intellectual,
was allowed to make speeches on such non-Thatcherite subjects as
the classics, philosophy and art history, but concluded:

> *Overall our strategy on higher education seemed right: expand
> student numbers in the polytechnics, rationalise the universities by
> concentrating some subjects in centres of excellence rather than
> having mediocre departments on every campus,[14] put more empha-
> sis on teaching and encourage both sides of the binary line to be
> more entrepreneurial by setting up science parks and the rest. But
> our rhetoric made it too easy for the universities to claim that we
> were a bunch of philistines with no idea what universities were for,
> and there was no lack of Tory MPs to reinforce that suspicion.*

---

13. Denham and Garnett, *op.cit.*, pp. 391–3.

14. On this see Shattock, *op. cit.*, ch. 3.

*'Why don't we just make them give up this Shakespeare nonsense
and do something useful?' was the contribution to policy I received
from one backbencher.*[15]

Walden later admitted:

*Our policy seemed to replace a selective system by a mass system –
the opposite in many ways to what we were trying to do in the
schools. And of course it was mass cultivation on the cheap. Ever
more students herded into ever expanding institutions to graze,
untutored, on ever thinner pastures. Ever more 'higher' education
based on the insecure foundation of chronically inadequate schools,
whose poverty of aspiration and anti-elitist resentments seemed a
poor preparation for 'higher' studies!*[16]

In 1987, Walden resigned, cynically observing that his lasting contribution was that he 'helped to cut the unit of resource by several
per cent.'

During the Thatcher years, while the numbers at universities
remained almost stationary, the numbers in the public sector – on
the other side of the binary divide – continued to grow. By 1987, of
those in higher education roughly fifty per cent were by then in the
public sector. The leading polys were anxious to become universities, while in the university sector there were those who felt some
of their number should be demoted to the public sector. (Keele was
a favourite example.) The attitude was underlined by Norman

---

15.   George Walden, *Lucky George* (London, 1999), p. 270. He even took Alan Bloom, the
author of *The Closing of the American Mind*, to see Margaret Thatcher 'in the hope of infect-
ing her with an enthusiasm for non-utilitarian studies which she lacked', *ibid*, p. 273.

16.   *Ibid*, p. 289.

Tebbit, a right-wing confidant of Margaret Thatcher who, in 1984, threatened that universities that did not co-operate with government policies would be demoted to polytechnics.[17] Yet the claims of polytechnics were greatly strengthened by the White Paper of 1985, when it became abundantly clear that the main purpose of higher education was, in future, to service the needs of the economy.[18]

One of the ironies was that, as the polys grew, they began to move away from their early concerns with engineering and teacher education[19] (seventeen also incorporated art schools). In part the change was necessary: some of the heavy industries for which they had been created were in terminal decline. Law began at Manchester Poly in 1966 and rapidly became a major concern of the polys. By the late 1980s computing began to take off. Modern languages were taught, not in connection with literature, but often as part of a business course. By the 1990s, business was the largest subject, but many more had appeared. In the mid-1970s, recreation and leisure studies were introduced, together with sports studies; in the 1980s the allied medical professions – physiotherapy and occupational therapy, together with nursing – bloomed at the polys – as these groups sought to become graduate professions. The growing popularity of media studies, communication and related subjects was a source of scepticism for traditional academics. The polys adopted the American modular system and were much more willing to experiment with multi-disciplinary degrees than universities. The CNAA became more willing to approve graduate

---

17. Kogan and Kogan, *op. cit.*, p. 40.

18. DES, *The Development of HE into the 1990s* (Cmnd. 9524).

19. The so-called James Report (DES, *Education: A Framework for Expression*, 1972) calling for a graduate teaching profession effectively handed the training of teachers to the polys.

degrees, particularly in polys like Portsmouth, where research was thought of as important. Meanwhile other polys, such as Greenwich, developed access courses to 'make experience count'. Hatfield had courses designed for mature women; Central London for trade unionists.[20]

Whatever Mrs. Thatcher thought about universities, she did try to improve the quality of technical education. Compared with Germany and Japan, students in Britain left school younger; nevertheless, compared with Germany, there were fewer apprenticeships. The system of industrial training had largely collapsed under Labour's efforts to rationalise (or nationalise) it and it was also weakened by the rapid rise in unemployment. (By 1981, twenty per cent of young males were unemployed.) The Manpower Services Commission, favoured by Mrs. Thatcher, established the Youth Training Scheme in 1983, emphasising technical skills. The Prime Minister saw this as the key to Britain's economic success and a foil to the elitist attitude of the universities. A new quango was created, the National Council for Vocational Qualifications (NCVQ), to create a certificate programme, not necessarily restricted to the young. These certificates were to be highly practical evidence of skills learned and mastered on the job. It was touted as a way of 'upskilling' the workforce. The early euphoria in the eighties gave way to a sense of failure in the nineties, as Britain failed again to press the right button to educate its traditionally underskilled workforce.[21]

In the meantime morale in the universities continued to sink.

---

20.   Pratt, *op. cit.*, pp. 110–52.

21.   For a rather bullish report, written in 1987, see Peter Jenkins, *Mrs Thatcher's Revolution*, *op. cit.* at pp. 270–1. Contrast the more recent (and devastating) Alison Wolf, *Does Education Matter? Myths about Education and Economic Growth* (London, 2002), especially ch. 3.

The brain drain, especially to the United States, accelerated as academic salaries, especially for outstanding academics, became in relative terms, ever more derisory.[22] The national salary scale meant that universities were not able to respond to overseas offers; but the AUT remained firmly opposed to merit pay and to the government's proposals for more flexibility in salaries. Nor did the universities' fortunes change as the ministers changed. In 1986, Kenneth Baker replaced Keith Joseph. While Baker under New Labour became a supporter of universities, that was not how he was viewed during his time as Secretary of State for Education. Much of his prodigious energy and decisiveness was, it is true, devoted to establishing a national curriculum in the primary schools (in the secondary schools O levels – later GCSE's – set the tone) in an effort to repair damage done by 'progressive' educational philosophy. Baker – and Margaret Thatcher – had little time for the teachers or the teaching unions, which they, with some justification, regarded as associates of the 'loony left' and political correctness.

It was clear that the universities were not well run. The Jarratt Report in 1985 included an embarrassing list of management failures. At that time, however, there still seemed hope. The Jarratt Report, commissioned by the universities, observed:

> *The UK universities make outstanding contributions to our national life. Their ... degree courses are shorter than those of any other developed country and their wastage rate is low not least because of their emphasis on small group teaching and personal*

---

22. Peter Jenkins, *op. cit.*, pp. 273–4. Real earnings growth between 1981 and 1992 was: for male university teachers 8.6 per cent; for NHS nurses 29.4 per cent; for NHS doctors 34.5 per cent; for male primary and secondary school teachers, 35.0 per cent; for male fire officers, 39.4 per cent. David Watson and Rachel Bowden, *Ends Without Means: The Conservative Stewardship of UK Higher Education 1979–1997* (Brighton, 1997), p. 17.

tuition. They play the leading role in maintaining and advancing scholarship in the humanities and the social sciences, where their achievements are high by international standards. They carry out the greater part of pure research in the United Kingdom and much of the applied research on which the future scientific and technological development depends . . . They underpin in culture and the arts the quality of national life.

The universities, however, were soon giving Baker an opportunity to reorganize them too. In 1985 the government had appointed the Croham Committee to review the UGC's constitutional position,[23] on the recommendation of the Committee of Vice-Chancellors and Principals - as the current Vice-Chancellor of London University put it, 'in its classic posture of aiming a very powerful rifle at its feet and pulling the trigger'[24]. The Croham Committee found two major weaknesses. It thought first that there ought to be greater public control over the use of tax funds by universities – although it talked in terms of accountability. Second, it recommended that the UGC be given statutory status, that it be reduced in size and that, instead of having primarily academic members, the majority of members should be non-academics. The government was happy to oblige.[25]

At the end of 1986, the universities did receive a reasonable financial settlement as part of a Faustian pact between Secretary Baker and Sir Maurice Shock, Chair of the CVCP (then Vice-Chancellor of

23. *Review of the University Grants Committee* (Cm. 81, 1987).

24. Graham Zellick, *Universities and the Law: The Erosion of Institutional Autonomy,* (London, 2001), p. 7.

25. For the assertion that the government deliberately distorted the recommendations of the Croham Committee, see Maurice Kogan, 'Managerialism in Higher Education', in Denis Lawton, *The Education Reform Act: Choice and Control* (London, 1989), p. 67.

Leicester and later Rector of Lincoln College, Oxford). The government had demanded 'real progress in the development of the policy of selectivity, the rationalisation of small departments, better financial management and improved standards of teaching'.[26] In return, the UGC agreed to distribute research funds more selectively, it agreed the disciplines where small departments might be merged and agreed that tenure needed to be weakened.[27] Shock, on behalf of the CVCP, offered assurances on academic standards – foreseeing a quality agency, with universities ensuring performance appraisal, implementation of the Jarratt Report, and an acceptance that something had to be done about tenure.[28] These commitments led to the last serious increase in academic salaries. The deal allowed Baker to make his famous Lancaster speech where he proposed doubling the participation in higher education over a fifteen-year period to match the supply of graduates in the USA. In fact the number increased by a half between 1986/7 and 1992/3 alone, partly because more students had been encouraged to stay on at school by the replacement of 'O' levels by the GCSE. In 1985/6 there had been 909,300 students (596,100 full time) in higher education; by 1992/3 there were 1,408,800 (822,800 full time). A year later the number was closer to two-thirds greater. It was a remarkable development.

The earlier cuts, however, had weakened and antagonized the universities. The previously independent institutions deeply resented the attacks. Baker shared Mrs Thatcher's view that the universities were 'pushing out poison' and did not deserve more money to teach irrelevant subjects. The 1987 White Paper, *Meeting the Challenge*, left

---

26. DES, press release, 6 November 1986 ('Kenneth Baker announces more money for education').

27. Attachment, letter from UGC to Secretary of State, 4 November 1986.

28. Attachment, letter from CVCP to Secretary of State, 5 November 1986.

no doubt where they were going. Instead of the universities deciding what the liberal arts and sciences called for, 'a major determinant must also be the demands for highly qualified manpower, stimulated in part by the success of the Government's own economic and social policies'. There was 'an urgent need, in the interests of the nation as a whole, and therefore of universities, polytechnics and colleges themselves, for higher education to take increasing account of the economic requirements of the country'. The government and its 'central funding agencies' were committed to bringing 'higher education closer to the world of business'.[29] As Simon Jenkins observed: 'The world of business was seen by ministers, few of whom had any experience of it, in a golden haze: it was a vague amalgam of the free market, hostility to unions and sympathy to the Tory party.'[30] Whitehall would in future decide what the needs of industry would be and, in a phrase which sounded more like the Cuban five-year plan than the public reputation of Mrs Thatcher, the White Paper announced that 'if evidence of student or employer demands suggests subsequently that graduate output will not be in line with the economy's needs ...Government will consider whether the planning framework should be adjusted'.[31] Mrs. Thatcher's free-market cabinet loved it! They had destroyed the collegiate model and substituted the dependency model.[32] British Telecom and British Rail might be privatised; the universities were to be nationalised.

Moreover, Baker was prepared to go further than Croham. Whereas the Chobham Committee had recommended the continu-

29. Department of Education and Science, *Higher Education: Meeting the Challenge* (Cm.114, 1987).

30. Simon Jenkins, *op. cit.*, p.143.

31. Cm. 114.

32. See Kogan, *op. cit.*

ation of the block grant to universities, Baker abolished the UGC and replaced it with the Universities Funding Council (UFC) with a majority, not of academics, but of outsiders. The Council was directly accountable to ministers. In addition to the block grant the internal contract was proposed. In future the government would 'buy certain services from universities... The government will use the power which the situation gives it to press for higher quality and greater efficiency, just like Marks and Spencer'.[33] The contracts would be for one year; and money would be withdrawn if the services were 'inefficiently delivered'. These demands were ultimately modified after pressure in the House of Lords.

The sub-committees of the UFC assessing performance had difficulties. Was popularity clear evidence of teaching ability? Too often, in these early years, the number of publications became the criterion for research quality. The government was, as the economists would say, a monopsony; and it wanted universities to compete within the context of needs. Moreover the DES had reserved prerogative powers if any university stepped out of line or the Department decided to change the subjects being offered – indeed the reserve powers seemed to give the DES total control over universities (power again somewhat reduced after strong opposition in the Lords). Nevertheless, British universities were now clearly part of the state apparatus of education; they were part of the public services.

At least some of these proposals were implemented by Kenneth Baker in the 1988 Education Reform Act. That Act achieved the abolition of tenure for new appointees and those promoted. It was sold as a measure to enable universities to rid themselves of poor teachers and non-performing researchers. It was, however, a bitter

---

33.　Cited in Jenkins, *Accountable to None*, p. 144.

psychological blow to academics. Baker originally even refused to put an acknowledgement to academic freedom in the Bill. Only when the Bill looked as if it might be defeated in the Lords did the government accept an amendment by Roy Jenkins along these lines. John Griffith, a socialist academic from the LSE, compared the Act to the dissolution of the monasteries. Simon Jenkins commented: 'If a government cuts your income each year without cutting its expectations, you not only run out of money, you run out of autonomy.' What the government had promised as a badly needed review of management in the universities – the Jarratt Report – although actually commissioned by the universities, was used to destroy still further the independence and pride of the universities. Academics were apparently being punished for having failed to become 'one of us'. As Baker himself said, 'The academic establishment at the universities was the first professional middle class group whose practices and interests were challenged by the Thatcher Government.'[34] Civil servants, physicians and lawyers were to follow, although all proved tougher than Belloc's 'remote and ineffectual dons'. The fact that universities had become subject to a *dirigiste* system of central control was ignored by a Cabinet wedded to the market.[35]

There were changes too to the 'public' sector, the other side of the binary divide, by then with fifty per cent of students. The 1988 Act severed the link between polys and local authorities and gave them their own funding agency – the Polytechnics and Colleges Funding Council (PCFC). Now that the whole of the tertiary sec-

---

34. *Ibid*, p. 147.

35. Deepak Lal claimed that when Baker met his opposite number in the USSR, he was congratulated on centralising power over the universities just as the USSR was attempting to devolve power. Lal claims that part of the purpose of the 1988 Act was partly to protect the middle class's subsidy at the universities, partly to pander to the sixties dons who loved uniformity. Deepak Lal, *Nationalised Universities: Paradox of the Privatisation Age* (London, 1989).

tor was controlled by the centre it became easier to bring costs under control. Baker claimed that while only one in eight students went to university, Britain spent a larger proportion of its GDP on higher education than any Western country except the Netherlands. He also alleged that the cost per student was higher than in California, although California's GDP was twice that of the UK's. Baker's goals were clear. Talking of changes in the 'unit of resource' he complained that 'this formula became sacrosanct and meant that if student numbers were increased then the amount paid through the unit of resource had to be increased. Since the student/lecturer ratio was never questioned, this meant the cost of expanding universities was very high'.[36]

The answers seemed obvious to Baker. Having imposed the National Curriculum on primary schools, and having noted that the polytechnics had added to their numbers at lower marginal cost, the old university funding scheme was replaced by one which was more openly based on *per-capita* funding, with different rates for arts, science and medical students. Then there were increasing changes in the funding of students. Keith Joseph had failed to increase maintenance grants in line with inflation; Kenneth Baker abolished social-security (welfare) grants to students, which had previously supplemented the maintenance grants and, in 1989, began to substitute loans for grants.[37] The 1988 White Paper *Top-up Loans for Students* noted that the cost of maintenance grants had risen from £253 million in 1962/3 to £829 million in 1987. Moreover the number of full-time students was to rise by sixty-seven per cent between 1988 and 1993 as part of the Shock-Baker deal. Baker realised that at least part of the maintenance grants had

36. Kenneth Baker, *The Turbulent Years: My Life in Politics* (London, 1993), pp. 233–4.

37. Education (Student Loans) Act 1990.

to be replaced by loans. Loans helped the government on the maintenance front; the basic funding of universities remained in chaos
with decline as its central consequence.

By mid-1989, Baker was replaced as Secretary by John
MacGregor, who continued the Baker policy of favouring the polytechnics. As he explained, they had a 'track record in meeting
demand', they were dedicated to the 'learning of practical applications', with courses 'characteristically related to the needs of industry and commerce' and they brought 'the benefits of higher education to many who would not otherwise have enjoyed them'. Early in
November, MacGregor was replaced by Kenneth Clarke. At the
end of November 1990, however, Mrs Thatcher was toppled by
Tory rebels and John Major became Prime Minister. Margaret
Thatcher had done more than any other Prime Minister to destroy
the Newman view of the university. She was proud of her contribution to secondary education – Assisted Places, grant-maintained
schools and City Technology Colleges; but even she, looking back,
agreed she may have been too hard on universities. In her memoirs,
she boasted first about what had been accomplished:

> *By exerting financial pressure we had increased administrative
> efficiency and provoked overdue rationalization. Universities were
> developing closer links with business and becoming more entrepre-
> neurial. Student loans (which topped up grants) had also been
> introduced: these would make students more discriminating about
> the courses they chose. Limits placed on the security of tenure
> enjoyed by university staff also encouraged dons to pay closer
> attention to satisfying the teaching requirements made of them.*

In retrospect, however, Mrs Thatcher was more gracious and
admitted that some critics 'were genuinely concerned about the

future autonomy and academic integrity of universities: I had to concede that these critics had a stronger case than I would have liked. It made me concerned that many distinguished academics thought that Thatcherism in education meant a philistine subordination of scholarship to the immediate requirements of vocational training'. Somewhat disingenuously she announced, 'That was certainly no part of my kind of Thatcherism.' She added, 'that was why before I left office Brian Griffiths, with my encouragement, had started working on a scheme to give the leading universities much more independence. The idea was to allow them to opt out of Treasury financial rules and raise and keep capital, owning their assets in trust. It would have represented a radical decentralisation of the whole system.'[38] It sounded like the return of the UGC for the fortunate few. It was not to be.

---

38. Margaret Thatcher, *The Downing Street Years* (London, 1993), pp. 598–9.

5. *John Major and the End of the Tories*

The nineties were a sad end to the Conservative administration which began in 1979. Although returned again in 1992, the unceremonious ejection of Britain from the Exchange Rate Mechanism in September of that year destroyed the Conservatives' reputation for good economic management and left the party increasingly marginalised and divided. Nor was there a coherent view on universities. The Prime Minister, John Major, had not been to university and appeared not to be particularly interested in them, although he did use them for political purposes.

As we saw, in 1987 Kenneth Baker and the Treasury agreed that universities might recruit students on marginal fees. It was a politically attractive arrangement. Both Baker and the Treasury had assumed the universities would not rise to the bait, pleading that the increase in numbers would affect quality. Dons had frequently argued 'more means worse'. It turned out that both universities and polys were more interested in cash than quality. While the explosion may have helped the Tories win the 1992 election, the cost for the Treasury both in fees

---

1.   Gillian Shephard, Patten's successor, attributed Patten's lack of success to the fact that

and grants was horrendous. In 1993, the rather unsuccessful Education Secretary[1], John Patten, a former Oxford don (Geography, Hertford), was forced to cut the fee and reimpose control on numbers. This was followed by Kenneth Clarke's drastic budget cuts (he had gone on from Secretary of Education to be Chancellor of the Exchequer) again having an impact on higher education.

The later Conservative years saw other crucial changes. The student loan programme, begun in 1990, had helped to make further expansion possible. In 1993, the 480 further education and sixth-form colleges were freed from local control, giving central government immense power over the tertiary sector. In 1988, against the bitter hostility of the AUT, the national system of salaries was freed up, at least at its upper levels. In 1990 the average full professorial salary was higher in England than the US; it was just that the best were absurdly underpaid by US standards. In 1989, in a move that saved the major research universities in England, university block grants had their research and teaching components separated. Teaching grants remained *per-capita* grants, but research grants were to be more obviously based on merit. The research assessment exercise was by then sufficiently developed and while not always welcomed in the universities, in fact it proved a system which preserved centres of research excellence in the nineties. Ironically the policy of emphasising research support based on excellence appeared just as the funding of teaching was reduced to the egalitarian mean.

In 1994 the Higher Education Funding Council spawned its own quango – the Higher Education Quality Council – whose purpose was to monitor the quality of teaching in universities (there had always been a system of inspection in the polytechnics). In this sense

---

the Department of Education was not a 'hands on' department and was incapable of implementing the Baker and Clarke reforms, especially in primary and secondary education. Gillian Shephard, *Shephard's Watch: Illusions of Power in British Politics* (London, 2000), p. 23.

it mirrored the newly independent Schools Inspectorate for Primary and Secondary Schools. Originally initiated by the CVCP for fear the government might do something worse, it gradually fell under the sway of government, who appoint 'observers' (in 1997 it developed into the Quality Assurance Agency.)[2] While good reports brought no extra money to the universities, poor ones were bad publicity for the university concerned. The Department of Education by then effectively controlled not only most aspects of spending by the universities; it was able, through its quangos, to monitor all aspects of their teaching and research. The DES put pressure on universities to move to 'modular' courses (along American lines) and towards 'continuous evaluation', both interests of the DES civil servants.

The DES proudly pointed out that the universities were still treated as part of the private sector in terms of the government's accounts, and that made it possible for universities to borrow and to start spin-off companies. It was also, however, a political convenience since it meant that the cost of universities did not appear on the government's books, something that was important as Brussels took an increasing interest in national budgets. With greater freedom having been given to certain secondary schools, the tertiary sector was now, in many ways, more centralised and regulated than the primary and secondary sectors. This highly *dirigiste* system in turn led to allegations of cheating. There were clearly cases, although probably exaggerated in number, of students being miscounted: maths students were counted as science students, who attracted higher fees (of course paid by the government). Similarly there were professorial appointments geared almost exclusively to the research exercise, the name substituting for real contact with

---

2.   On these developments, see Roger Brown, 'The New UK Quality Framework', *Higher Education Quarterly*, vol. 54, (2000) p. 323.

the department.[3] Just as factory managers had learned to play the system in the USSR, deans and vice-chancellors operated the system in England.

John Major's most significant contribution to higher education, however, was to abolish the binary divide and to merge the polytechnics (and some other colleges) into the university sector. In the early eighties the polys had grabbed some of the power from the degree-controlling body, the CNAA. The CNAA was left primarily with quality control issues and those were later transferred to the HE Quality Council. Then in 1988, the polys were finally taken from under the control of local authorities and given their own funding agency. Finally, a remarkably casual White Paper, which read more like an executive summary than a serious analysis, was published in 1991,[4] saying that 'polytechnics' was not a term easily understood. It recommended that they be allowed to call themselves universities and to compete on equal terms with existing universities. Indeed in certain cases, colleges of higher education, some of which had recently been 'promoted' to polys,[5] were eligible to apply to become universities.[6] The polys wanted the change, overseas students wanted the change, it had political advantages for the Conservatives, yet it put Britain out of sync with most of Europe, where similar institutions have continued to thrive as learning centres for technological education.

---

3. Martin Trow, 'Trust, markets and accountability in higher education: a comparative perspective', *Higher Education Policy*, vol. 9, (1996) p. 309. See especially pp. 313–14

4. DES, *Higher Education – A New Framework* (Cmnd. 1541, 1991); Martin Trow, 'Thoughts on the White Paper of 1991', *Higher Education Quarterly*, vol. 46, (1992) p. 213.

5. The number of polys had remained constant at thirty from 1973. In 1989 Humberside was promoted; in 1990 Bournemouth; in 1991 Anglia; in 1992 West London, which became Thames Valley University later that year. During the nineties, the University of Gloucestershire, previously known only in the novels of David Lodge, was created out of higher education colleges in Gloucester and Cheltenham.

6. This latter opportunity was basically the history of the Universities of Derby and Luton.

The PCFC – the Polytechnics and Colleges Funding Council – established in 1988 to fund the 'public' sector, was merged with the UFC (the Universities Funding Council) – the replacement for the UGC – into a new umbrella organisation, the Higher Education Funding Council (HEFC). Major himself saw the change as attacking snobbery;[7] and Kenneth Clarke, the new Education Secretary, a bluff barrister with a rumpled Rumpole style, delivered the appropriate legislation in 1992. In retrospect, a Conservative Minister of Higher Education called the change 'another example of how class consciousness has decided educational policy'.[8] Many Tory ministers had doubts; none had the courage to oppose the merger, and it passed unopposed in Cabinet. It was, moreover, difficult to deny that the polys had made a vital contribution.[9] Yet the decision had more to do with inflated expectations, the need to keep up the supply of foreign students – an essential part of the export drive and by then a vital element in the funding of higher education – and ministers' egos as they looked at comparability statistics of university graduates in OECD reports. Names might change; the reality did not necessarily do so.

In general what became known as the new universities were delighted with their enhanced status. Directors became vice-chancellors, sometimes better paid than their peers in the old universities. They welcomed being members of the CVCP (the Committee

7.   John Major, *The Autobiography* (London 1999). The book includes a Major aphorism of the kind which so delighted *Private Eye*: 'Only in Britain could it have been thought a defect to be too clever by half.'

8.   George Walden, *We Should Know Better: Solving the Education Crisis* (London, 1996), p. 189.

9.   In 1992, there were 272,400 mature students in polys, 57,200 in universities. Universities were 92 per cent white, polys 86 per cent (4 per cent black, 9 per cent Asian). Total numbers in the polys had gone from 169,741 in 1965/6 (full-time 21,788, sandwich 10,042, part-time day 23,169, part-time evening 21,921) to, in 1992/3, 454,809 (full-time 187,668, sandwich 76,592; part-time day 87,394, part-time evening 27,115) - Pratt, *The Polytechnic Experiment* (Buckingham 1997) pp. 26, 66, 73.

of Vice-Chancellors and Principals), being able to nominate persons for honours – a quaint British custom – and being invited to garden parties at Buckingham Palace.[10] Principal lecturers might become professors; deans were everywhere. To their staff, being able to claim research funds from the Research Councils on an equal basis was an important breakthrough. At the same time the new universities were to discover that, since the research element of the block grant was distributed on merit, their pickings were normally slim. Overall, the government had other reasons for liking the arrangement. Historically, polys had operated on a far lower basis of funding than universities. The latter's expectations were in the process of being brought down to the poly level. There was now one standard of support.

The collapse of the binary system in 1992 was not accompanied by a Master Plan like the California system; any university might give any degree. There was not to be a hierarchy like the University of California, the California State University and the community colleges.[11] The typical poly was normally based on a merger of the local technical college, the local teacher-training college and the local art college; but their histories were sometimes very different. As their status changed, some saw themselves, at least in part, as

---

10. 'Vice-chancellorial vanity' was the expression of John Pratt, historian of the polys. He recently argued that 'there is a question of whether they would have been better off as first-class polytechnics than second-class universities'. He argued that while they may have acquired the title of university, they lost the support of the PCFC and the CNAA. 'Status, more than just a name', *Times Higher Education Supplement*, 20 September 2002. Other critics have argued that the art schools are losing their creativity as they are being absorbed into the university system and having their teaching built around degrees. Andrew Lambirth, 'Quick-fix solutions', *Spectator*, 24 May 2003, p. 49.

11. After an initial interest in the 1990s by HEFCE and the Department, interest in the California system and the Michigan system declined, presumably because they allowed wide diversity among institutions and were drifting towards privatisation. There was a growth of interest in the Wisconsin system, presumably because there was less diversity, less distinction and more central control.

competitors with the older universities: Oxford Brookes University and the University of the West of England are perhaps the most obvious examples. Such universities took on the middle-class patina of the older and contiguous universities. Some polys consciously clung to their original purpose as primarily centres of technical education and applied research, closely associated with local industry and occupations: these included the University of Derby, South Bank University and Southampton Institute. Some had outstanding departments, like architecture and media at the University of Westminster or aeronautical engineering at the University of Hertfordshire. Nottingham Trent ran what was regarded as the best professional training programme for lawyers in the nation. Liverpool John Moores University and Leeds Metropolitan had outstanding programmes in sports sciences, Oxford Brookes in history. Some of the new universities existed at the margins of the tertiary sector – the University of North London, Thames Valley University, the University of Luton, the University of Wolverhampton. Some, such as Bournemouth University, had virtually no research profile.

The British, who had long sneered at American higher education because it was so academically diverse and so practical, now had a vast array of new universities, with a significant number of students doing not only media studies and tourism, but applied engineering and fashion. Suddenly there were institutions offering programmes in Caribbean Studies, Beach Management and even Yorkshire Studies. The University of Northumbria had an Associate Degree in Call Centre Studies – call centres by then being the fastest-growing sector in the British economy. Liverpool John Moores had a BA in pop music; Plymouth in Surf Sciences and Technology; Luton a BA in advertising. The older universities sometimes followed suit:

at Birmingham it was possible to do a degree in Golf Management. The academic and applied diversity of American institutions had arrived; it was, however, subject to a system of bureaucratic centralisation which made a mockery of real diversity, yet without any clear vision which might have provided some rationality.

As Simon Jenkins observed:

> *Nothing better symbolized the standardization of British higher education than this uniform application of the word 'university'.*
>
> *The reason for this decision appears to have been twofold: to double Britain's 'university' population at a stroke, and to bring all teaching and research under a single planning aegis. The end of the polytechnic appeared a clear victory for the university, as the monopoly supplier of higher education in Britain. Yet in my view it was not the university but the polytechnic that triumphed. The constitutional status of the British University had been shattered. In its place was Baker's concept of a work-oriented, vocational, commercial institution, run more like an externally accountable public corporation than a collegium of scholars. This concept was essentially that of a polytechnic. The local-authority sector may have lost the war, but it won the argument. The polytechnics had not become universities. The universities had become polytechnics.*[12]

Jenkins's idea was not original. Eric Robinson, one of the early proponents of the polytechnics, had argued in 1968 that:

> *Sooner or later this country must face a comprehensive reform of education beyond school – a reform which will bring higher education out of the ivory tower and make it available to all.*

---

12. Simon Jenkins, *op. cit.*, pp. 151–2.

This will be achieved through a bloodier battle than that for the comprehensive reform of secondary education. In that battle the grammar school was the victim. In the next, the victim will be the university – the commanding height of British education. The shape and speed of this change to come depends upon the success with which the polytechnics are established.[13]

By 1992, it seemed that Robinson's vision was all but achieved. The only difference was that the battle had not been bloody; the universities went like lambs to the slaughter. The strongest universities could resist the slide. Oxbridge, the leading London colleges and strong 'provincials' like Manchester and the leading Murray universities like Warwick retained many of their features. They continued to offer primarily single-subject honours degrees in largely 'academic' subjects. They did not accept the modularisation approach. Even they, however, became obsessed with links with industry, transfer technology and the like. At its best, of course, this was desirable, but in the hands of many of the 'old' universities talk of links with industry too often sounded like the incantation of the belief that universities existed primarily to increase the GNP. This had the effect that while the new universities felt they knew their role in society, the less prestigious of the old universities seemed to have lost their sense of direction. What indeed was the future of Keele and Sussex, Leicester and East Anglia? Would they survive the squeeze between the best ex-polys and the leading old universities?

As the polys were absorbed into the university sector there was increasing interest in developing practical instruction in skills which would be of immediate value to UK industry. As the univer-

---

13. Eric E. Robinson, *The New Polytechnics* (London, 1968), p. 10.

sity sector had grown by leaps and bounds, especially during the nineties, the industrial apprenticeship system had largely collapsed and it was difficult to see what had replaced it. (In fairness an apprenticeship in one industry may not have been the ideal training for a rapidly changing economy). As early as 1986 the National Council for Vocational Qualifications had been established and shortly thereafter the National Vocational Qualifications appeared. They were designed to give parity of esteem with academic qualifications, but too often NVQs were dismissed by students as 'No Value Qualifications'. Nevertheless, by 1996 there were 180 lead bodies defining 'standards of competence' for different jobs and 794 different kinds of NVQ. The 'New Apprenticeship' had been born – although only about forty of the 800 NVQs were extensively used. The Conservative government, as NVQs faltered, invented the NCVQs, between A levels and NVQs, as usual, highly controlled from the centre. They tended to be taken by students who could not make it via the A level route. The NCVQs became 'vocational A levels'[14] as the result of yet another Dearing Report.[15] Sir Ron (as he then was), bowing to industry, refined 'core skills' to 'key skills' and the strange, centralised, story of the redefined modern apprenticeship had begun the next leg of its journey.[16]

Higher education itself limped towards the end of Conservative rule in 1997. By 1995 the Student Loan Company – set up by the government to handle the loan scheme because the British commercial banks did not have the imagination to run it – was on the verge of collapse. The new 1992 universities – varied as they were

---

14. Alison Wolf, *op. cit.*, ch. 3: 'A great idea for other people's children: the decline and fall of vocational education'.

15. SCAA, *Review of Qualifications for 16–19-Year-Olds* (1996).

16. Wolf, *op. cit.*, pp. 124–5.

– continued to enjoy their new status. It was the pre-1992 universities that suffered most. A few thrived. Oxford and Cambridge continued to receive not only a block grant from HEFCE but college fees paid in full without a means test by the LEAs. Understandably this was a system which was a cause of friction with some other universities and generated a feeling of serious hostility among the egalitarians in the DES. After George Richardson's reforms of Oxford University Press, the university benefited from the immense commercial success of OUP, while Cambridge had a strong income flow from its examining enterprises. Warwick thrived through the entrepreneurial activities of its Registrar.[17] The London School of Economics under its Director, John Ashworth, who had revolutionised Salford after its funds were dramatically cut, sought to impose a top-up fee at the LSE. The faculty, motivated by muddled notions of equality, failed to support him. The LSE increasingly solved its financial problems by taking a majority of full-paying overseas students. Universities (and the financially weaker Oxbridge colleges) effectively underwrote UK (and later EU) students by packing in overseas students. Thanks to Mrs Thatcher, or perhaps Shirley Williams, overseas students paid the real cost of their education. Many universities had links – and first-year colleges – in developing countries: Derby in Israel,[18] Swansea in Malaysia and Cardiff in Nigeria.[19] That was the path increasingly followed by old and new universities. Their income was also

---

17. Such success naturally infuriated academics, see E. P. Thompson (ed.), *Warwick University Ltd* (Harmondsworth, 1970).

18. In 2003, Derby was in trouble with the QAA for admitting underqualified students into its programmes in Israel. 'QAA finds Derby broke quality rules overseas', *Times Higher Education Supplement*, 23 May 2003.

19. And when Nigeria imposed exchange controls in the mid-eighties, Cardiff went into serious financial difficulties. Shattock, *op. cit.*, ch. 6.

increasingly supplemented by taught masters programmes for some of which, illogically, market fees were charged for all students including those from the UK – the more the better. Rube Goldberg or Heath Robinson would have been proud of this arrangement.

In retrospect some of the Tories' changes were inevitable. The English tax system could not bear the burden of expansion at the level of the best. The Major government insisted on efficiency gains each year, normally at the level of one per cent; at Oxford, as the College fee was cut, they amounted to three per cent. The 'unit of resource' fell by forty-seven per cent during the Conservative years. Too often it seemed that civil servants in the Education Department were happy with the philosophy of the unions – the National Union of Teachers and the Association of University Teachers (and later the unions from the other side of the binary divide) That philosophy held that equality, even if it meant mediocrity, was better than excellence if that involved social inequality. Civil servants discouraged changes in policy that they believed might be meritocratic, just as they had done in the Wilson years.[20]

The remarkable achievement was that between 1979 and 1997 the number of college-age students going full-time to universities rose from 510,000 to 1,100,000.[21] At the same time the amount the government paid the universities per student had been cut in half. There were, by then, eighty-seven universities and forty-seven higher education colleges. The faculty-student ratio fell from 1:9 to 1:17; and even at the best universities, there was a gradual decline in the quality of education. At the less fortunate institutions, there

---

20. Baker, *op. cit.*, pp. 166–8

21. The number of part-time students rose from 267,000 to 518,000. In addition there were 1,750,000 part- and full-time students in the further education colleges. Of these, forty per cent were doing A levels; the remainder worked towards degrees, NCVQs and qualifications such as the City and Guilds.

was more rapid decline. What was perhaps most interesting was that, during the Major years, the middle class became dramatically more 'uni'-minded than before (the gruesome word 'uni' achieved widespread acceptance after the 1992 merger). Fifty-five per cent of the children in social class I and II (professional) had gone to university in 1991/2; in 1995/6 it was seventy-nine per cent. In social class V (unskilled) the relevant figures were six per cent and twelve per cent. The potential for conflict was considerable.

Late in 1995, with the universities increasingly in financial difficulties and, because of the Patten cap, no longer able to plug the gap by pushing in more students, Leslie Wagner, the Vice-Chancellor of Leeds Metropolitan University, proposed that all universities impose a £300 top-up fee per student. Gareth Roberts, the Vice-Chancellor of Sheffield, who was the Chair of the CVCP, was prepared to stand firm and support the move.[22] Gillian Shepard, who had replaced the unfortunate Chris Patten, then colluded with Labour to set up a committee (the Dearing Committee) on the funding of higher education to report after the impending election (eventually held on 1 May 1997). It was tacitly agreed that university funding, and especially fees, would not be mentioned during the election campaign.

---

22. He had earlier suggested that the V, C and P stood for 'Vacillation, Chaos and Procrastination'.

Part II

New Labour and the Universities:
1997–2003

6. *Themes of the Nineties*

Looking back from 2003 and the new White Paper on higher education, there is now widespread acceptance that the 137 institutions of higher education are underfunded, probably to the tune of £3 billion annually, with a £9 billion deferred construction and maintenance bill, and the need for a further £3.6 billion if Britain wants a fifty per cent enrollment in higher education.[1] It is curious to reflect on why the nineties were a period of drift. There are a number of reasons.

The most important reason was that the articulate middle class regarded the universities as their personal part of the Welfare State,[2] and the upper-middle and middle class maximized that par-

---

1   The House of Commons Education and Skills Committee calculated that a fifty per cent participation rate would require 17,000 more academic staff. *Post-16 Support*, HC 445 (2002), para. 48.

2.   'People who showed little interest in the standards of schools they did not use, and who were disinclined to exert pressure either for better teachers or better resources, were more sensitive to what happened in the institutions of higher learning that their children progressed to after their independent schools. Here was a high-quality, generously funded state service, delivered free of charge (i.e. no tuition fees) to rich and poor alike, to which the social and moneyed elite (by whom its best institutions were disproportionately used) had become understandably attached. Of all the universal benefits available to the upper classes higher education is the only one for which no private substitute is available (outside our only independent institution, the University of Buckingham) and which no amount of money can buy.
   'It was all part of the unspoken British educational settlement. The psychology behind it – insofar as it was conscious – was not unreasonable. Having already dug deep into their pock-

ticular hand-out in the 1990s. Discussion of the universities' funding problems might lead to the recipients of the remarkable largesse actually having to pay more. The massive expansion in higher education had been funded at the expense of universities (especially the older universities), whose budgets for teaching were cut dramatically, and at the expense of academics, whose salaries barely increased in real terms and whose work load escalated as the faculty-student ratios declined. Knowledgeable parents had a good idea that the quality of English universities was on the decline – but reputations, as it is said, are always ten years behind reality, and providing Johnnie was enjoying himself, 'why bother?'. The facts that universities now received per student roughly as much as a comprehensive received and one quarter of what they had paid for Johnnie at a fancy public school was ignored. The residential nature of the English universities – particularly the older ones – provided Johnnie with a pseudo-public school experience which gave, if not an academic experience, at least a social one and the sceptic might suggest that socialisation was increasingly the apparent purpose of higher education. (English students, unlike American ones, expect the universities to provide single rooms; at Oxbridge they expect servants.) If you are feeding free at the trough it may be unwise to complain about the food.

Astute politicians also knew what was going on, but no MP after the Keith Joseph fiasco was going to suggest any change in funding; indeed when Jeff Rooker, the Labour spokesman on higher educa-

ets to keep their children out of maintained education, while simultaneously paying for the children of others through their taxes, when it came to higher education people felt no compunction about exploiting to the maximum, the best the state could offer. You could purchase a place for a bright child at Eton, but not at Oxford – though it was by paying for it at Eton that you stood a better change of securing the place at Oxford. That was (and to an extent still is) how the wheel turned. The fact that a high-quality service benefited those at the middle and lower levels of society was incidental, though a handy alibi for the continuation of a free system.' George Walden, *We Should Know Better* (London, 1996), pp. 169–70.

tion, floated the idea of a graduate tax, he was fired. George
Walden, a former Higher Education Minister, put the position
astutely:[3]

> *The danger of over-stretching the capability of institutions to*
> *absorb extra students was not unforeseen when expansion was dis-*
> *cussed in the mid-eighties. It would be a simple-minded*
> *Government who thought you could cram in more students indefi-*
> *nitely without risk to quality. (The hope was of course that stan-*
> *dards in school would rise in parallel.) Only market romantics*
> *seriously believed that, by a combination of belt-tightening, better*
> *management, better teaching with modern methods, and attracting*
> *private money and foreign students, the value of a University*
> *degree in a hugely expanded system could continue unimpaired.*
>
> *There were other kinds of romantic: those who affected to*
> *believe (or still worse did believe) that the Treasury would simply*
> *find the money from the taxpayer, and that expenditure per pupil*
> *could continue at its previous high rate in a system tripled in size.*
> *Such people comprised a wide political spectrum, ranging from the*
> *liberal-left to the upper-class beneficiaries of a totally state-fund-*
> *ed system. Here was another of those unlikely* de facto *alliances*
> *one stumbles across in British politics. Both leftist and patrician*
> *had a joint interest in letting expenditure rip – the only difference*
> *being that, if he had his way, the leftist would seek to recoup the*
> *money by raising the taxes paid by the patrician.*
>
> *To sober-minded people on all sides of Parliament the solution*
> *to the financial problems of our universities has been obvious for*
> *some time, though such is our system that sobriety and politics are*
> *frequently incompatible. Open discussion of where the money was*

---

3.   Walden, *ibid*, p. 122.

to come from was impossible during the entire period of expansion, and remains so till this day. To all intents and purposes Parliament has side-stepped the issue entirely.

The idea that one might be training an educated elite who would provide leadership in different areas of life had become politically unsustainable. It was much easier to say the more graduates there were the richer the country would be and, in a circuitous argument, the fact that they earned more was assumed to be conclusive proof that they were making the country richer. Best to ask no questions.

Why did the university community not speak out? There were so many reasons. Partly the state of primary and secondary education seemed so dire.[4] Many would have privately agreed with Sir George Mason, the former Vice-Chancellor of UMIST (The University of Manchester Institute of Science and Technology) who opined: 'The decision to expand higher education before attending to the schools was like adding an extra storey to a house with crumbling foundations.'[5] There was an even broader problem. Many comprehensives, especially in the inner cities, were a failure educationally (there were beacons of success including some of the schools the Conservatives had allowed to opt out and the technology colleges).

Perhaps the biggest, if undiscussed, problem was that secondary education in England took place in a yobbish culture. It was not just the ethos of the soccer hooligan or towns where it is impossible to walk on Friday and Saturday evenings because of the clubbing and pubbing crowd. Britain has for its teenage generation the worst

---

4.   Charles Clarke, Secretary of State for Education and Skills, recently told the House of Commons Committee on Education and Skills that if he were 'bold and radical ... I would not put any money into universities and I would put all the money into nurseries and primary education ... to change educational disadvantage in this country'. Evidence, 19 March 2003.

5.   Cited by Walden, *We Should Know Better*, p. 171.

crime rate in Europe and the worst statistics for unmarried pregnancies, drugs and alcohol. It also has the worst illiteracy rate. Only some forty per cent of the cohort of social classes IV and V achieves five grades of C or above in the case of GCSE subjects and, while cross-cultural comparisons are always hazardous, that is roughly the equivalent of graduating from an American high school. Roughly one-fifth of the whole British population is functionally illiterate, according to the Moser Commission on Education. If politicians had sought to make some sense of the schools before turning their attention to the universities, it would not have been entirely surprising, nor unreasonable. The fact that they did not put the universities on the defensive.

Nor were the universities articulate. The Association of University Teachers was a largely ineffective trade union. It did call strikes – normally about pay – but the sight of a few bedraggled and ill-clad faculty members on the evening TV news scarcely engendered fear or sympathy.[5] The AUT, and its more radical union confreres who had emerged from the polys, were committed to the egalitarian philosophy of Old Labour. Merit was out; research suspect. The unions and many of their numbers did not come out of a tradition where universities were regarded as independent centres of thought. They regarded themselves as another group of ill-paid employees of another public service.

The logical mouthpiece for the universities – the Committee of Vice-Chancellors and Principals (renamed Universities UK early in the new century) – was not effective. It had not always spoken with one voice before 1992; after 1992 it was so diverse and the interests it represented were so different that it was difficult to agree on anything. It was not that they disagreed about top-up fees

---

5.   E.g. 'Lecturers strike for city pay allowances', *Evening Standard*, 14 November 2002.

or a graduate tax; they could not even agree to ask the government for more money. Attempting to bridge the gap, they appointed as their Chief Executive Diana Warwick, a former official with the NUT, later General Secretary of the AUT. She brought to her new job the commitment to an egalitarian system and a left-wing bias. Indeed in 1999, in the kind of move that can only happen in England, she was made a Labour peer in the House of Lords, while retaining her CVCP post. She continued to harangue Parliament in a way that was sometimes antithetical to so-called international or research universities.[6] The policy of the universities' trade union appeared to put equality well ahead of excellence.

Meanwhile the international universities failed to give leadership. At Oxford and Cambridge, endowments and the college fee meant that dons were largely sheltered from the cruel economic winds that swept across the remainder of higher education. When the Conservatives in the mid-nineties were willing to let Oxbridge charge top-up fees, a possibility which might have made such fees politically possible for the whole university sector, as well as giving Oxford a serious amount of freedom, Oxford refused to do anything which might disturb the college fee.[7] Indeed the Report of Oxford's Commission of Enquiry in 1997 concluded that 'Oxford should aim to remain part of the UK's publicly funded system of higher education'. To privatise even the sums received from HEFCE would involve the 'unrealistic target' of £2 billion. (In fact, in those heady days of initial public offerings, Oxford University Press could prob-

---

6.   See speech by Baroness Warwick of Undercliffe, *Parl. Deb.*, vol. 641, col. 758 (27 November 2002), speaking in favour of the equality of universities, the need to remain dependent on government funding, opposition to top-up fees, scepticism about research, etc. To American nostrils, the speech smelt of a commitment to mediocrity.

7.   See 'An Open Letter to the Chairman of the North Commission', *Oxford Magazine*, Second Week, Hilary Term 1997, p. 2. (Drafted by Peter Minfield and the author.)

ably have been floated for appreciably more than that.)[8] To go private, said the Report, would take one hundred years.[9] No government had much to fear from that approach.

With few exceptions, there were no obvious leaders among the vice-chancellors of any of the leading universities, nor could they rely on the support of their academic staff for any radical positions. The majority of vice-chancellors knew full well that the system, which in fifteen years had tripled in size with only half the traditional level of funding, could not continue. Yet in the bureaucratic system in which the universities operated, vice-chancellors were reluctant to step out of line or to speak out of turn. Max Weber would have enjoyed the implications of a group who appointed one another to committees and were consulted on the allocation of honours – to one another. As George Walden, the former Higher Education Minister, remarked of the universities, 'Far from exercising their joint authority to call all sides to order and to appeal for a grown-up debate on the financial future of their institutions, they kept their heads well up in the clouds and their feet planted firmly on shifting sands.'[10] *The Times* even went so far as to describe the vice-chancellors as a 'hot house of cold feet'.

In fairness, compared to the United States, it was not easy for universities to take strong positions. American universities are top-down institutions: while there is active faculty participation; they leave strong executive power in the hands of presidents and boards of trustees. As a generalisation English universities are bottom-up institutions. While varying greatly, staff or faculty play a far more vital part in executive decision making and Councils, where they exist,

---

8. In 2003, OUP made a capital gift to the university of £74m.

9. *Commission of Inquiry Report*, University of Oxford, 1997, paras 12–16.

10. Walden, *We Should Know Better*, p. 175.

tend to be weak. The political views of academic staff are therefore significant and there had been a move to the left in their views over the decades.[11] Academics, much as they might resent the short changing of universities by the Conservative government, were not about to abandon the centralised funding and micro-managing of universities to which they had become accustomed. Moreover the vice-chancellors and senior professors were an integral part of the committee structure which made the *dirigiste* system work. The absence of a sense of outrage, part of the national character, and the British tradition of muddling through, played into the hands of a government that had effectively nationalised and homogenised the universities. Not surprisingly, along with the majority of citizens, most academics voted to oust the Conservatives in 1997.

---

11. For the beginning of this process, see A. H. Halsey and M. A. Trow, *The British Academics* (London, 1971), ch. 15.

7. *Dearing and the First New Labour Administration*

As the 1997 election approached, neither party was anxious to address the issue of university funding. The Conservatives were proud of their record on keeping public spending down — after all they had doubled the number of universities, tripled the number of full-time undergraduates and more than halved the amount the government put into a unit of resource, as students had become known. They could proudly point to the eighty-seven universities and forty-seven higher education institutions in the United Kingdom. They knew that the universities were grossly under-funded and they also knew that the quality of education, particularly at the pre-1992 universities was sinking, if not dramatically, at least steadily. New Labour shared this knowledge. All agreed that more money was needed in the sector, but Old Labour (and the fragility of the partnership between Old and New Labour was hidden after 1997 by the collapse of the Conservative Party) took some delight in the slow demise of the old universities.

As the election of 1997 approached, however, both parties were conscious that the underfunding could not be remedied by the Treasury

alone in a time when increased taxes were out of fashion. At the same
time neither party wanted to face Middle England, which not only
provided crucial votes in general elections but also contributed to the
overwhelming mass of students in the university sector and enjoyed its
remarkable subsidies. Their votes were assiduously cultivated not only
by the Conservative Party, but also by New Labour.

There was therefore tacit agreement that the ball would be kicked
into touch. During the election there would be no mention of maintenance grants or loans, fees imposed by the government or top-up
fees (as fees imposed by the universities had become known). Instead,
another committee, under Sir Ron Dearing, had been established
with a broad remit to consider 'how the purposes, shape, structure,
size and funding of higher education, including support for students,
should develop to meet the needs of the UK over the next twenty
years'. It was 'support for students' that was the key and Sir Ron was
the man for the job. A lifelong bureaucrats' bureaucrat, he had served
as Chairman of the Post Office Corporation and Chairman of the
Universities Funding Council. He had chaired various 'quickie' committees on education and he was given a committee of educators and
businesspeople, but the committee was shaped by the Department for
Education, who set much of the tone of the Report.

It is perhaps unfair to criticise a Report which was intended to
avoid serious discussion of the future of higher education. *Higher
Learning in the Learning Society*[1] was published in July 1997, two
months after New Labour was returned in a landslide.[2] It was undistinguished as a Report about the future. Indeed, the Report, whatever one's views on higher education, is primarily noteworthy for being

---

1.   *The National Committee of Enquiry into Higher Education*, 1997.

2.   David Butler and Dennis Kavanagh, *The British General Election of 1997* (London, 1997).

3.   For a strong critique, see Duke Maskell and Ian Robinson, *The New Idea of a University*
(Thorverton, 2001), ch. III/4 'The Vision and the Mission'.

written in the platitudinous verbiage now traditional in educational writing.[3] It substituted exhortation for thought: 'We recommend that, with immediate effect, all institutions of higher education give high priority to developing and implanting learning and teaching strategies which focus on the promotion of students' learning'.[4] Perhaps only a Committee without any practising academic on it could produce such an insight. With its provenance and style it was not surprising that the word 'university' was scarcely mentioned. With the platitudes out of the way,[5] the Report got down to what lit-

---

4. *Over the next 20 years, the United Kingdom must create a society committed to learning throughout life. That commitment will be required from individuals, the state, employers and providers of education and training. Education is life enriching and desirable in its own right. It is fundamental to the achievement of an improved quality of life in the UK.*

    It should, therefore, be a national policy objective to be world class both in learning at all levels and in a range of research of different kinds. In higher education, this aspiration should be realised through a new compact involving institutions and their staff, students, government, employers and society in general. We see the historic boundaries between vocational and academic education breaking down, with increasingly active partnerships between higher education institutions and the worlds of industry, commerce and public service. In such a compact, each party should recognise its obligations to the others.

    Over the next 20 years, we see higher education gaining in strength through the pursuit of quality and a commitment to high standards. Higher education will make a distinctive contribution to the development of a learning society through teaching, scholarship and research. National need and demand for higher education will drive a resumed expansion of student numbers – young and mature, full-time and part-time. But over the next two decades, higher education will face challenges as well as opportunities. The effectiveness of its response will determine its future.

That future would require higher education in the UK to 'encourage and enable all students whether they demonstrate the highest intellectual potential or whether they have struggled to reach the threshold of higher education – to achieve beyond their expectations.'

    This last suggestion was discussed at 5.57. As students with 'more modest prior academic attainments or abilities [are admitted] adaptations to programmes and qualifications will be needed'. That appeared to be a clarion call for dumbing down. In a 2003 survey, seventy-six per cent of academics claimed that they had been forced to 'adapt' their teaching techniques for the changing student body. Some sixty per cent admitted they had 'dumbed down' their teaching. 'Dumbing Down rife, poll reveals', *Times Higher Education Supplement*, 23 May 2003.

5. See also Martin Trow, 'More trouble than it's worth', *Times Higher Education Supplement*, 24 October 1997; and 'The Dearing Report: A Transatlantic View', *Higher Education Quarterly*, vol. 52, (1998) p. 93. And see also Anthony O'Hear, *The Dearing Report: A Personal Response* (London, 1997).

tle meat it contained. The first half of the menu was a reflection of the interests of the bureaucrats in the Department for Education as it was by then known. First and foremost was the establishment of an Institute for Learning and Teaching in Higher Education. No faculty member in future should be appointed to a substantive position without having a teaching certificate from this body. Indeed the Secretary of the Committee, a Department for Education bureaucrat, announced that what would distinguish English universities from those in other countries was that lecturers in England would all have teaching certificates. Then there was to be a much-enhanced QAA (Quality Assurance Agency) which would supervise 'programme specifications' for each course in every university and supervise franchising arrangements (many English universities by then survived by running programmes in developing countries – for profit). There was, however, the suggestion of 'light touch' reviews as the new Institute for Learning and Teaching came into being. In addition the QAA was to be given power over standards and qualifications throughout the higher education sector.

In particular standards would be maintained by the QAA establishing a pool of 800 external examiners who would ensure standards throughout the higher education sector. How this was reconciled with the diversity in the sector, also in principle embraced by the Report, was unclear. How does one ensure that Greats at Oxford has the same standards as the course on the Spice Girls at Honiton College? Indeed, since the Report was packed with systems of external control, there was almost no sense that universities might be autonomous institutions. Single-subject degrees were frowned on, anything savouring of an Ivy League rejected; 'continuous evaluation' and modularisation were the order of the day. Since employers demanded it, all courses should be linked to the 'world of work'. All courses, whatever their subject, were to include the 'key skills' – communication, numeracy and IT.

To complete the atmosphere of *Brave New World* the Report announced that 'Young People entering Higher Education will increasingly come with a Progress File which records their achievements up to that point and which is intended for use throughout life. We favour the development of a national format for a transcript of achievement in higher education which students could add to their Progress Files'. As they progressed through higher education, the degree would be replaced by 'levels attained' – H1 being the first-year certificate and H8 a doctorate. The last jab, inserted by the Department for Education bureaucrats, was to demand a review of the Oxbridge college fees (the additional subsidy paid by LEAs to those universities).

Strangely, the Report's main proposal, reflecting its main purpose, was not followed. The Report, in what was apparently a compromise at the end of the Committee's deliberation, called for grants and loans to be repaid, not gradually after graduation, but through a system of repayment which only kicked in when income reached a certain level – the so-called contingent loan scheme. At the same time the Committee also recommended that students should contribute roughly twenty-five per cent of the cost of their education by way of a fee, again to be paid after university when their income reached a certain level. The new government, however, already showing cracks, chose to go its own way. The Chancellor, Gordon Brown, having taken a vow to stay within the Conservatives' spending formula, was faced with Kenneth Clarke, the last Conservative Chancellor, having cleverly inserted various back-end cuts in his 1995 autumn Budget statement to take effect only after the election. With that background Brown refused to give the Education Secretary (David Blunkett) the interim funding that would be needed to keep the system going until the recommended post-university payments kicked in. The new Secretary of State was therefore forced to bring in up-front fees of some £1000; this was means tested, so that only roughly one-third of students paid the full fee and one-third a reduced fee. Maintenance grants, however, disappeared; all student support was to be through interest-free loans, with repayments beginning when earnings reached £10,000 p.a.

To some extent this apparently aberrant decision reflected the structure, attitudes and rivalries of New Labour. While a proportion of the massive number of new Labour members were part of the modernisation known as New Labour, probably the bulk of the backbench Labour MPs were Old Labour. While the modernisers had taken over the leadership of the party, its finances were still significantly provided by the unions. If, over the following years, there was not a coherent policy, that is understandable. Old Labour despised selection, the basis of admission at the universities. The days when Harold Wilson could boast he had eight Oxford firsts in his Cabinet had passed. So-called elite institutions were out of favour. Old Labour hated the Conservatives' policy of opting out at the secondary level (which allowed some state schools to be selective) and it wanted all universities to look as much alike as possible. It was committed to the comprehensive principle at the high-school level, even if that forced London Labour MPs to send their children to comprehensives which they knew to be grossly inadequate.[6] The typical Labour MP increasingly looked to the universities to

---

6.   When Tony Blair wanted to bring into the Labour Cabinet legal luminaries who had children at private schools – people like Charlie Falconer and Peter Goldsmith – they were, or had to be created, peers rather than expected to find seats in the House of Commons. They would never have got through Labour constituency party selection committees. In 2003, Andrew Adonis attracted criticism for even enquiring about a child attending a fee-paying school where instruction was in German.

redress the inadequacy in the schools. Mass higher education – with as much uniformity as possible between the universities – must be the solution.

Even within the modernisers in the Labour Party, however, there were dramatic differences. In 10 Downing Street was Tony Blair, a muscular Christian and a clever politician. His chief adviser was Peter Mandelson – known to the bulk of the Labour Party as the Prince of Darkness – together with Alastair Campbell, a former political editor from a downscale newspaper and a master manipulator of the news. On most issues, it seemed for the first four years that the Prime Minister's chief interest was in Labour's having a second term. Certainly there were issues on which Tony Blair had strong and principled feelings – making peace in Northern Ireland and intervening in the horrendous civil war in the Balkans. On most matters, however, his administration appeared as a government of spin. Philip Gould – a disciple of Bill Clinton's dubious spin doctors – ran focus groups and organised initiatives. Indeed, initiatives and targets were the order of the day. In secondary education there were targets for reducing the number of disruptive students excluded, and in primary schools for reaching a certain level in the three Rs. If there was too much truancy, set a target. If too much traffic congestion, set a target. In the health service, there were goals for reducing waiting lists for surgery and increasing the numbers of mammograms. Sometimes such initiatives worked. More frequently they distorted some other queue. As Charles Goodhart sagely observed, when government statistics are incorporated into government policy, they are invariably open to misuse.[7] It

---

7.   In its original form: 'any observed technical statistical regularity will tend to collapse once pressure is placed upon it for control purposes'. C.A.E. Goodhart, *Monetary Theory and Practice: The UK Experience* (London, 1984), p. 96.

took some while for New Labour to realise that initiatives and targets were a poor substitute for policies, but that was after various
initiatives and targets had been introduced to attempt to ensure
more state school students went to the leading universities.[8]

The Treasury is more powerful in Britain than it is in the United
States. Responsible government provides few checks and balances
and the Treasury not only runs the economy but also has immense
power over the spending departments. Effective power over budgets therefore resides with the Chancellor of the Exchequer rather
than the Prime Minister. It was natural that Gordon Brown should
be Chancellor, the head of the Treasury. He was a consummate
politician, with wide experience in the Scottish Labour Party.
Many, including Gordon Brown himself, believed that he, rather
than Tony Blair – regarded by some in the Party as an effete public-school Oxbridge type – should have been Prime Minister. While
Brown and Blair agreed, when John Smith died suddenly, that
Brown would not oppose Blair as candidate for Leader of the party,
many thought that it had also been agreed that halfway through the
second term – in mid-2003 – Brown would replace Blair. Relations
between Brown and Blair were not good, although probably, at least
in the early years, not as bad as portrayed in the press.

Brown has proved an excellent Chancellor. The British economy,
at least until recent months, has thrived compared with its rivals.
Gordon Brown has, however, not given up his interest in replacing
Tony Blair and that has had its influence in the ongoing debate
about higher education.[9] While Brown has favoured the enterprise

---

8.   'The trouble with targets', *Economist*, 28 April 2001.

9.   To achieve his leadership goal, he has been required to keep his power base in Scotland
sweet and thus it has been necessary to retain the Barnett formula. This forces the English taxpayers to provide more generous educational and health benefits in Scotland and Wales than
in England: indeed such benefits are twenty-three per cent higher per head than in England.

economy – an almost Thatcherite view of the market[10] – his cultivation of Old Labour has meant that, in many areas, he talks an
egalitarian line and plays to the class battles of Old Labour. He
insists the market solution must stop at the boundaries of education
and health.[11] His position appears to be that it is more important to
have equality than excellence in health services and in education
(including the universities). Ironically, the Treasury's policy for
funding university research is, by these lights, highly elitist.
Brown's biggest disadvantage in succeeding (or deposing) Blair,
however, is that in an era when charisma is thought to be essential
in a politician, Brown lacks it. His second disadvantage is that he
despises the badges of the English middle class, from dinner jack-

---

This has meant that Scotland has been in a position to fund its universities more generously
than England, while it has far more money to fund the Scottish NHS, to pay its teachers better and to provide free nursing home care, without imposing the 3p income tax it is allowed
under devolution. 'Port on the menu!', *Economist*, 27 July 2002. Ironically, the author of the
scheme, Lord (Joel) Barnett, Chief Secretary to the Treasury 1977–9, later said Scotland was
receiving far too much money: 'I didn't know it would last all these years. I thought it was a
temporary expediency…there was no proper needs assessment…[it] was purely political … It
was started on a single population basis to save me a bit of trouble.' It now means that GDP
in the north east England is £9,473 p.a., in Scotland £10,975. 'Scotland gets far too much
money', *The Times*, 23 June 2000.

10.   The enterprise concept is in some ways skin deep. While there is much talk of encour-
aging entrepreneurs, the atmosphere in business reflects much more a command economy
than in the US. Government and business are much more involved with one another, and the
state has a wide range of weapons to direct industry and commerce.
   Of course, there are areas where the market has 'let rip'. Captains of industry now command
salaries and 'packages' comparable with their US peers. The privatised industries provide similar perks. The City provides salaries and bonuses comparable with Wall Street; and leading
accountants and lawyers live well. Soccer players live even better. Even the Civil Service, well
paid by US standards, has 'merit' pay.
   Having said that, the bulk of the English economy still looks like the planned economy of
fifty years ago. Throughout the public services – including the NHS, teachers and universities
– there are national salary scales. Efforts to make the system more flexible are vigorously resis-
ted. Even in the private sector the national salary is the norm, negotiated with a single union.
Labour economists are still wont to imply that the mega salaries should be ignored and the rest
of society should opt for the egalitarian approach. Tony Atkinson, 'The tall story of widening
inequality', *Financial Times*, 16 August 2000.

11.   Bagehot, 'Life after Tony', *Economist*, 15 March 2003.

ets to residential universities; yet, to be elected, a party needs the votes of this very group.

One of Brown's chief rivals for the succession is David Blunkett, a remarkable politician, blind from birth, who grew up in Sheffield politics and later took a degree at Sheffield University. (Tony Blair was at St John's, Oxford, and Gordon Brown at Edinburgh.) Blunkett as Secretary of Education until the 2001 election at once showed that he was a man of the people, as well as a person of courage. He readily saw that the primary schools were in need of moving back to basics and that, at the secondary level, so many of the comprehensives were failing. He followed the initiative model, but was willing to stand up to the unions where necessary and was willing to experiment in the provision of secondary education. One suspects that, like Tony Crosland, he was not particularly interested in universities. (His most famous remark was that his son, studying science at Liverpool University, was neglected by his teachers, who were too busy doing research.) He nevertheless showed courage in forcing through the changes in universities even if they were misconceived. One suspects the main voice on universities was the Higher Education Minister, Baroness Blackstone, the former Master of Birkbeck College in the University of London.

8. *New Labour in Action: 1997–2001 Reconsidered*

New Labour rushed into office in 1997, charged with a commitment to change. There were so many things to reform. For a while there was much talk about the rebranding of Britain. As usual, however, higher education was low in the list of Government priorities. New Labour's response to the Dearing Report was to ignore its advice on funding.

Baroness Blackstone was not, however, about to ignore one piece of advice in the Report relating to college fees at Oxford and Cambridge. *De facto* these two universities double-dipped because both the university and the colleges charged fees and, as part of the compromise on overseas fees, the government paid both. It was an understandable source of irritation to some other universities, not to mention to the bureaucrats in the DfEE, who resented the lack of uniformity represented by the independent colleges in those two federal universities. Tessa Blackstone was reported to have wished to be a Foreign Office Minister, where she could dismantle the Foreign Service, to which she had taken a dislike when she was in the No. 10 Policy Unit. When she was instead made Minister for Higher Education it is said that she declared that at least she would console herself by fixing Oxford and Cambridge; and she did her best.[1] After limited analysis, HEFCE recommended the phasing out of college fees. The Chancellor (the titular head) of Oxford, Roy Jenkins, rallied the troops and lobbied hard. The college fee did go, but Oxford became eligible for a new programme: Old Buildings grants – technically available to any university but in fact intended for the two oldest. The result was that Oxford and Cambridge lost only a third of their teaching income. (In many ways, however, the bureaucrats in the Department achieved their goal: in future the money would be paid to the university rather than the colleges, signalling the beginning of the end of the college system). The real blow for all universities came when Tessa Blackstone inserted into the Act the right to make illegal the power to charge fees. While this need was primarily aimed at Oxford colleges, its breadth meant that all universities had by then been truly nationalised.

In the spring of 1999, the depth of tribal hatreds became clear when Gordon Brown attacked an admissions decision of Magdalen College, Oxford with respect to Laura Spence. Brown had many of his facts wrong; while the applicant was a good student, there were better – including minorities and state school students. (She had applied to Magdalen to read medicine, but went to Harvard to study for a BA in natural sciences.) Yet Alastair Campbell was not dissatisfied, because Brown had 'got a controversy up'.[2] In no time John Prescott was attacking Newcastle and Durham Universities for their admissions policies, although they had both offered Laura

---

1.   Robert Stevens, 'Eviscerating Oxford', *Spectator*, 14 July 2001, p. 22.

2.   Andrew Rawnsley, *Servants of the People* (London, 2000), p. 379. The 'facts' were developed by Labour's reelection team at Millbank. Brown's actual remarks were: 'It is about time we had an end to that old Britain when what matters to some people is the privileges you were born with rather than the potential you actually have. I say it is time these old universities open their doors to women and people from all backgrounds.' James Naughtie, *The Rivals* (London,

Spence admission to read medicine. Robin Cook, the Foreign Secretary, joined in by saying he was going to discriminate against Oxbridge graduates in entrance to the Foreign Service, an odd announcement at the moment Oxford was making prodigious efforts to attract state school students. While Tony Blair said 'let's hear no more rubbish about class war', the silliness went on. Mo Mowlam, the Northern Ireland Secretary and a graduate of Durham University, said on the television programme *Room 101*, 'I hate people from Oxford – they talk posh.' Baroness Jay, Leader of the House of Lords, went to Washington and told Oxford alumni that the university was elitist and a 'problem'. (Washington was a city where the good Baroness was less well known for her expertise in higher education than for her spectacular affair, while married to the British Ambassador, with a *Washington Post* investigative reporter, later immortalised in a novel by Nora Ephron *Heartburn*, 1983.) Later, Robin Cook attacked the new Tory leader, Iain Duncan Smith, because his son had won a scholarship to Eton, the most famous of the public schools. The Conservatives responded by attacking the Prime Minister, whose son went to a (free) Catholic school across London which had opted out of state control under the Conservative government (an arrangement which allowed it to use modified selectivity), and was being coached for A levels by a master at a public school, Westminster!

2001), p. 273. Brown has always hated Oxbridge – *ibid.*, p. 275. The main force of his attack fell on the President of Magdalen, Anthony Smith, a supporter of New Labour, thought by many to be about to be tapped for a Labour peerage. For a thoughtful analysis of his views, see Anthony Smith, 'The Laura Spence Affair', in Stephen Prickett and Patricia Erskine-Hill (eds.), *Education! Education! Education!* (Thorverton, 2002), p. 29. See also Anthony Smith, 'The lesson Labour should learn from Laura Spence', *Daily Telegraph*, 21 April 2001; William Rees-Mogg, 'This is the true scandal of Laura Spence', *The Times*, 28 May 2000; Ben MacIntyre, 'Organic Oxford and the Harvard Henhouse', *The Times*, 27 May 2000. In apparent support for Brown, see the observations by the Labour educational guru Sir David Watson (Vice-Chancellor of the University of Brighton) in David Watson and Rachel Bowden, 'Can We Be Equal and Excellent Too?' (Brighton University, 2001), p.14.

The English (and I include for this purpose the Scottish) politicians on class are tiresome in the extreme. They would be paralysed by the last American presidential election when the four leading contestants (Bush, Gore, McCain and Bradley) had all been to Ivy League institutions and three of them to preparatory schools (the equivalent of English public schools). Such an attitude also paralysed any reasonable approach to the academically distinguished universities in England.[3] Constant underfunding meant the leading universities, by then nestled in the Russell Group (so named because meetings were held in the Russell Hotel in Bloomsbury), were gradually declining in importance, at least when compared with the Ivy League. The views of a wide swathe of the Labour Party, coupled with the reluctance of the middle and upper class to pay for the education of their children at such institutions, made it appear that that decline was to be permanent.

Certainly with the decision on funding settled, and the end of the right of universities to charge fees, it very much looked as if it were business as usual. Managing decline was the order of the day in higher education. Under New Labour the cuts in university funding were in fact mitigated, particularly with respect to research, but overall the underfunding in higher education continued. The new universities, many of whom had been kept on a shoestring by local authorities, who ran them until the 1980s, adapted better than the old universities to the continued short rations. Yet central control, and standardised rates for teaching,

---

3.   The most obvious criterion was the size of the endowment. Only Oxford and Cambridge had serious endowments putting them (just) within the top twenty American universities, and far behind the leading Ivy League institutions. What most distinguished them was that, at least at Oxford and Cambridge, the colleges (the preponderant holders of the endowment) used the endowment income primarily for maintenance of buildings and subsidising the cost of room and board for students. American universities use a far higher percentage for teaching and research.

meant increasing homogenisation. It also meant declining flexibility and autonomy. With the generally acknowledged – although controversial – decline in the demands and standards for A levels,[4] universities were allowed to extend their science degrees from three to four years. Yet as students increasingly arrived less well prepared at the universities, the solution for law and medicine which US universities arrived at between 1920 and 1950, of having those as graduate subjects, was not available to English universities, because they were effectively controlled by the Treasury.

The willingness of the university sector to respond to the changing political world was limited. The amorphous nature of the CVCP had led, as we saw, to the emergence of the Russell Group – a ginger group of the leading research universities – while even it frequently failed to speak with one voice. (The Coalition of Modern Universities emerged as the voice of the former polys.) The Laura Spence affair ultimately led the Russell Group to commission the Greenaway Report on Higher Education,[5] contrasting the inability of English universities to decide on the number of their own students, let alone the right to charge fees, compared with Ivy League competition. The remarkable thing was that, during this period, access changed little, in spite of strengthening centralisation, continuing funding

---

4.   In some areas, the curriculum became less demanding, e.g. mathematics in the physics course, comprehensive coverage in history; but the challenge of the A level was probably chiefly devalued by the growth of 'continuous evaluation'. In 1989, 11.4 per cent of students got As at A level. By 2001 it was 18.6 per cent. 'A-level pass rates best for 50 years', *The Times*, 16 August 2001. For the decline in modern language A levels, see Frances Beckett, 'Dumbing Down', *Guardian Education*, 5 November 2002. Maths A level is to be made much easier in 2004: 'Hard Numbers', *Economist*, 19 April 2003. A study at the University of Coventry showed that what was a fail grade in maths A level in 1991 is now a B, *id*.

5.   David Greenaway, 'Funding Universities to Meet National and International Challenge' (Nottingham University, 2000).

cuts for teaching and increased bureaucracy. In the Major years (1990-7) the proportion of children from unskilled families going to university rose from six to fourteen per cent; the proportion of children from professional families rose from fifty-five to eighty per cent.

The issues of access and government funding thus became inseparable. As the leading universities' customers had remained predominantly middle and upper class, the amount spent on each student had declined dramatically since 1985 (when, in 2000 money, it was £8,500 in the universities and £4,750 in the poly-technics) to an average in all universities – old and new in 1997 – of £4,790.[6] Meanwhile, as we saw, the student-staff ratio had dropped from 9:1 in 1980 to 17:1 in 1998. By 2000, then, English universities had a worse faculty-student ratio than US universities. While the decline in funding for research was halted, New Labour was faced with serious problems.

Among these problems was academic salaries. Academic salary increases had fallen well below the average for non-manual staff.[7] In the OECD, English universities still scored well in terms of teach-ing and graduation rates; it was clear that German and French uni-versities were deteriorating even more rapidly than UK ones. (A point never discussed was that the economies of these two coun-tries appeared, until recently, to have thrived despite the decline.) Following Dearing, additional money was put into research

---

6.   The unit of public funding in 1988/9 had been 103 in universities and 75 in polys. By 1990–1 it was unified, with 100 in both. That rapidly declined to 76 in both by 1996/7. David Watson and Rachel Bowden, 'Ends Without Means' (Brighton University, 1997), p.15.

7.   In US/UK terms in 1992, the pay of assistant professors in the US had been 177 per cent that of lecturers. By 1997 it was 190 per cent. Greenaway, *op .cit.*, p. 34. Between 1981 and 1982, the real earnings growth of non-manual men rose by 37.1 per cent; that of male univer-sity teachers, 8.6 per cent. Watson and Bowden, *op. cit.*, p.17.

through the Joint Infrastructure Fund and the Joint Research Equipment Initiative. Since, with respect to research, both the block grant and grants through the Research Councils were based on merit, the decline in research was less obvious. In teaching, however, Britain lagged in international comparisons. With the funding for students cut by fifty per cent by 1997, among OECD countries, only Finland, Poland and the US had a higher percentage of students going on to higher education. At the same time average expenditure per student in the UK ($7,225) was only sixty per cent of the OECD average of $12,018. Indeed, Britain's overall expenditure on education (0.7 per cent of GDP) was the lowest in the OECD. Twelve per cent of British students were from overseas, and their contribution through fees to the survival of the UK universities was impressive, although it probably should have been embarrassing.

The university sector was slowly forced to think about its future. The Russell Group's Greenaway Report confirmed the figure of £400,000 as the lifetime average additional income earned by a graduate. The National Child Development Study suggested clear links between a degree and participation in community affairs and democratic values. Greenaway found the cross-country comparisons compelling: there was an association between education and economic growth with higher education being most significant. Since New Labour had committed itself to a fifty per cent participation rate in higher education (later transformed into a commitment to fifty per cent in further education), Greenaway examined how higher education might be funded in the light of the commitment to access. One way would have been to restore the unit of resource to its earlier more generous figure, but this would have required some £3.6 billion per annum; even to bring it to the OECD average would require a further £3.1 billion. A further £5.9

billion would be required to expand universities to take fifty per
cent of the age cohort. It was in this context that Greenaway exam-
ined the options: the graduate tax, the voucher, the unfortunately
named top-up fees, and a programme of deferring payments
through scholarships and income-contingent loans. These four
possibilities became the agenda for the higher education debate as
the new century dawned.

While New Labour had done little to reverse the Conservatives'
lack of investment in higher education,[8] the Prime Minister was
insistent that the tertiary sector had an 'incalculable impact on the
economy at large'.[9] The new Blunkett-instituted fees originally went
to general support of the tertiary sector, but even when they were
later directed to the universities which charged them, they had little
real impact, as the direct government subvention was reduced.
Meanwhile the net of bureaucracy was closing. While some of the
worst aspects of Dearing were ignored, the institute to train academics to teach was established – by 2006 no one will be eligible to teach
in universities without the appropriate certificate – and a College of
External Examiners was in the offing. The Quality Assurance Agency
for Higher Education was busy moving from institutional audits[10] to
subject reviews to academic reviews – although in the spring of 2002
the Russell Group succeeded in getting the most intrusive aspects of

---

8.   Another important document in this period was Howard Glennerster, 'United Kingdom
Education 1997–2001' (LSE). Perhaps the most interesting aspect of this paper is proof that
investment in education actually fell in the first New Labour administration.

9.   Romanes Lecture, Oxford, 1999.

10.   The best known institutional audit in this period was that of Thames Valley University
in November 1998, which reported that 'academic standards and the quality of students' experience' was under threat. Of the 27,000 students, two-thirds were part time, one-third in further education. Among modular courses available were curry making and kite flying. *Times
Higher Education Supplement*, 8 November, 2002, p. 8. And see Roger Brown, 'The New UK
Quality Framework', *Higher Education Quarterly*, vol. 54, (2000) p. 323.

its reports killed.[11] The Bett Report recommended more pay for academics, but suggested an even more *dirigiste* system with a single national pay scale and a National Council to negotiate pay and conditions. The Committee might have saved its breath; the government refused to fund the Report.[12]

In the meantime, as the continued 'efficiencies' for universities shrank available funds, academics began to notice. At Oxford the cuts in the college fee began to affect the poorer colleges, although the boom in the stock market protected the wealthy colleges.[13] (Such financial discrepancies made it increasingly difficult for the colleges to present a united front either to university or government.) Tutorials at Oxford and the supervisions at Cambridge were threatened by the financial changes and by the attraction of research, which was far better funded and professionally increasingly more prestigious. Developments such as these encouraged a serious debate regarding the state of the universities in the press. Martin Wolf at the *Financial Times* lobbied hard for American solutions – paying the faculty properly and allowing universities more

11. 'University standards reports to be scrapped', *Daily Telegraph*, 21 March 2002. John Randall, the head of QAA, had resigned the previous summer when the changes were mooted – 'University standards chief quits over cuts', *Daily Telegraph*, 23 August 2001. For the argument that there should be an even more intrusive system of accountability, see Roger Brown, 'Accountability in Higher Education. The Case for a Higher Education Audit Commission', *Higher Education Review*, vol. 33, (2001) p. 5.

12. The Independent Review of Higher Education, Pay and Conditions chaired by Sir Michael Bett was published on 23 June 1999. The government did make a small grant available to universities which produced a system of performance-related pay: HEFCE, 'Rewarding and Developing Staff in Higher Education' (OO/56, December 2000). Most universities have distributed this in as egalitarian a way as possible. See Gavin Williams, 'Fiscal Policy and Academic Salaries', *Oxford Magazine*, fourth week, Hilary Term 2001, p. 7.

13. Aggregating both university and college endowments, Oxford and Cambridge still appeared wealthy compared with other universities. 'Oxbridge reaps college premium', *Financial Times*, 2 April 2001. Again it must be borne in mind that much of the income from college endowments is used primarily to subsidise undergraduate room and board rather than academic programmes.

independence.[14] In this he was joined by a small group of academ-ics.[15] The majority of academics – at least in the old universities – seemed uninterested or vaguely optimistic that some government would come along to return the universities to the heady days of the UGC.

Indeed, it was outside the universities, in the archaic and strangely constituted House of Lords, that the most serious discus-sion about universities took place. In December 1999, Lord Jenkins of Hillhead initiated a debate, beginning with his usual refrain that 'this country is lucky enough to possess two old universities which have maintained their position in the world league much better than have the ancient foundations on the continent of Europe'. He then attacked the shrinking unit of resource and the idea that 'hav-ing pushed the number of universities up to over 100, you must then allow them to advance only in one equal and even line', argu-ing in favour of differential fees and need-blind admissions. He finally warned the government that it could 'not have it all ways: no extra public funding; no ability to raise charges. The result of that, gradually but inevitably, would be no first-class British universi-ties.'[16] It was left to the Bishop of Durham to express concern, 'when we hear talk of the universities' role in driving the economy, and of translating ideas into wealth and marketable opportunities, I

14.   E.g. Martin Wolf, 'Empty Chairs', *Financial Times*, 6 July 1999 ('Unless the Government tackles the stagnation in real pay of academics, the UK will become an intellectual backwater'); Wolf, 'Let the top universities off the funding leash', *Financial Times*. 6 March 2000; 'Why Blair should keep university tuition fees': "Giving in to the middle-class outcry will neither increase access nor solve the lack of funding for the tertiary sector", *Financial Times*., 6 September 2001.

15.   Robert Stevens, 'Top up fees required to save universities', *Financial Times*, 5 April 2000; Terence Kealey, 'Academics can never be free while the state foots the bill', *Daily Telegraph*, 12 July 2001; David Cannadine, 'Making History Now', Institute of Historical Research (University of London, 1999).

16.   *Parliamentary Debates* (House of Lords), vol. 607, col. 1284 (8 December 1999).

wonder whether we are in danger of getting our priorities wrong and are undermining the idea of a university given to the purpose of developing whole mature people who are able to live and take a lead in the complex set of demands which make up modern society'.[17] Lord Annan and Baroness Warnock regretted the end of the binary divide; everyone regretted the gross underfunding of higher education and the increasingly perilous state of the research universities. Baroness Blackstone offered but bland thoughts on behalf of the government.

Six months later, in June 2000, Lord Baker (Kenneth Baker that was) instituted another debate. The tone this time was more shrill. The Laura Spence affair had intervened and it was increasingly apparent that while the typical university was in financial troubles, the hope that the leading universities might compete with American rivals was dwindling. Although Lord Baker neglected to mention his own contribution to the decline, he noted: 'When great institutions decline, they do not decline precipitously: there is no precipice. They simply decline very slowly. Higher education in this country is now heading down that slope.' He concluded:

> *No government of any complexion – whether Conservative, Labour or a coalition – will ever provide the funds that are properly required for higher education in our country. Our universities are, in fact, a nationalised industry. They have all the characteristics and weaknesses of a nationalised industry. It is an underfunded mass system with national salary negotiations instead of regional and local salary negotiations; top-down regulation of student numbers and of courses in each university; incessant bureaucratic, trivial intervention, day-by-day, which the univer-*

---

17.   *Ibid*, cols 1308–9.

sities resent; and under-investment in libraries, laboratories and computer rooms.

Universities started as private institutions and they should become private institutions once again. They should become independent, free-standing bodies, totally in charge of their own affairs.[18]

For the government, Baroness Blackstone largely ignored the Laura Spence affair, pointing out that sixty-five per cent of those who gain three A's at A level were at state schools, but 'only 52 per cent of entrants to Oxford came from state schools and colleges'.[19] This statistic did not take into account (and the government irritatingly refused to keep numbers) that in the state schools there is a significant tendency at A level to take the general studies paper and subjects such as media studies, business studies and law, which are not regarded as appropriate subjects for admission to an academic university.[20] There was, however, an undertone of threat. Outside the House, Lord Puttnam, who had moved from making movies to being one of 'Tony's cronies' and overlord of teachers, explained that Oxford and Cambridge had had their college fees cut because they 'had behaved so badly'.[21] Baroness Blackstone was proud of the fact that New Labour was cutting university budgets by only one per cent a year – or at least only requiring a one per cent efficiency gain – but she was also threatening on the issue of independence. She warned that if

---

18.   *Parliamentary Debates*, House of Lords, vol. 613, cols. 1642, 1645 (14 June 2000). Lord Baker had some strange supporters, including the Labour peer (and LSE Professor of Economics) Lord Desai, who also advocated independence for universities. *ibid.*, col. 1707.

19.   *Ibid.*, col. 1722.

20.   The two fastest-growing A levels are media studies and sports studies. Meanwhile 46,000 took A level physics in 1989; 33,508 in 1998. O'Hear, *op. cit.*, pp. 8 and 9.

21.   *Parliamentary Debates*, House of Lords, vol. 613.

universities declared themselves independent, they would not only lose teaching funds, but access to government research funds.[22]

Laura Spence would not go away.[23] HEFCE began publishing tables to 'out' the most socially elite universities.[24] The subject never discussed in polite society, whatever the failings of the leading universities, was the abysmal academic standards in too many state schools. New Labour's policy, as always, was to have more 'targets'. The universities which exceeded their targets for social inclusion were Central Lancashire, Huddersfield, Teesside and Wolverhampton – institutions which came close to having open admissions and had horrendous drop-out rates. They were also sometimes the universities subject to 'holdback' by HEFCE – in other words, in this *dirigiste* life, they were the institutions punished for failing to meet their minimum number of students.[25] The elite universities responded by spending increasing sums recruiting from state schools and on combating the hostility – especially to Oxbridge[26] – on the part of many teachers in the comprehensive

---

22. *Ibid.*, col. 1721.

23. Anthony Smith, 'The lessons Labour should learn from Laura Spence', *Daily Telegraph*, 25 April 2001; 'Oxford still failing to attract state pupils', *The Times*, 2 April 2001. 'Seven universities judged too middle-class', *Daily Telegraph*, 6 October 2000. They were judged, by HEFCE, not to be admitting enough state school students or enough students from the lowest socio-economic classes or students from 'low participation neighbourhoods'. The seven were five old universities (Bristol, Exeter, St Andrews, Reading, UCL) and two new universities (Oxford Brookes and West of England). Ten others – including Oxford and Cambridge – failed on two of the three criteria.

24. 'Degree of elitism persists at universities', *The Times*, 6 October 2000. Peter Lampl, 'The scandal of bright children turned away by our top universities', *The Times*; 29 November 2000; 'One rich man against the system', *ibid.*

25. Higher Education Statistics Agency, *Students in Higher Education Institutions 1999/2000* (Cheltenham, 2001).

26. Oxford, not always wisely, has, over the last decades, made various efforts to become more accessible to state school students. First, it abandoned entrance exams normally taken in the third year of the sixth form. Then it abandoned entrance exams, illogically leaving the more subjective admissions interview. Finally, and especially after the Laura Spence fiasco, the colleges put intense efforts into outreach in the hope of interesting state school students in Oxford.

schools. A philanthropist, Peter Lampl, sought to raise the sights of underprivileged students as they considered university, at the same time arguing that the wealthy should pay full fees.

By this time, the House of Commons Select Committee on Education and Employment issued its report on access:[27]

> *We recommend that those institutions which do not reach the benchmarks established by HEFCE should come under particular scrutiny and should be encouraged to learn from best practice elsewhere in the higher education sector. Where an institution significantly underperforms its benchmark, it should be required to publish action plans on its strategies to widen access.*

While the Committee threw further doubt on the Oxbridge college admission system and wanted admissions to be done by specially trained interviewers, it refused to discuss Gordon Brown's attack on Oxford or John Prescott's attack on Durham.[28] That reluctance gave the impression that attacking the so-called elite universities took precedence over integrity in the world of New Labour.[29] While

---

27. House of Commons, Select Committee on Education and Employment, *Fourth Report* (3 January 2001).

28. *Ibid*, dissent by Evan Harris MP.

29. 'Yet the committee still proposed measures that assumed the existence of ranks of state-educated geniuses refused access to the best universities by an impenetrable old boy network tightly bound by old school ties.' – from 'Degrees of Bribery', leader, *Daily Telegraph*, 8 February 2001. See also Anthony Smith, 'A shoddy plot to save Gordon Brown's face', *The Times*, 7 February 2001; 'Universities should be paid to take low grades', *Daily Telegraph*, 8 February 2001. There were already incentives: '£151m incentive to recruit poor', *Times Higher Education Supplement*, 15 September 2000. On Oxford admissions, see also Evan Harris MP, 'Higher Education: A Question of Access' in Prickett and Erskine-Hill (eds.), *op.cit*, p. 39. Comprehensive students now account for 23 per cent of Oxford's intake, who, instead of the usual three As, have two As and a B. For independent schools the figure is 17.2 per cent. Increasingly, students from the public schools are expected to have four A levels.

the Committee came out against quotas for state and deprived-area students, its plans for incentives and punishments appeared to achieve much the same thing. Remarkably the Committee also refused to question the government's judgement by looking at the impact of student debt and the abolition of the maintenance grant.

One of the ironies of this period was the cult status that American universities appeared to achieve in the British mind. Gordon Brown gave money to the University of Cambridge to involve MIT in marketing the universities' scientific discoveries, something which had been going rather well – at Cambridge and elsewhere – without government assistance.[30] (It was said that Cambridge was chosen by the Chancellor partly to punish Oxford for Laura Spence; certainly the government auditor later criticised the Treasury for failing to follow open procedures in awarding the grant.)[31] Margaret Jay, the Leader of the House of Lords and an ex-wife of an ex-ambassador to the USA, discussed the Oxbridge admissions 'problem' at a commemorative occasion in Washington, announcing: 'You have done it at Harvard and Yale. We should do it at Oxford and Cambridge.'[32] The only problem was that Oxford has a far better access record than Yale in admissions. In the autumn of 2000, Oxford took 42.5 per cent of students from the seven per cent of students at independent schools, and 48.2 per cent from state schools, which overall have 93 per cent of students. Yale took 32 per cent of its students from the prep and

30.   Commentators frequently overestimate the amount that American universities generated from the industrial exploitation of their research and similarly had unrealistic expectations about what English universities might gain. Thomas Barlow, 'Universities and the facilities for making a profit', *Financial Times*, 9-10 June 2002.

31.   'Cambridge upbeat despite criticism', *Times Higher Education Supplement*, 23 May 2003.

32.   The good Baroness was not helped by her claim to have attended the local grammar school when in fact she had attended a Girls' Public Day School Trust school. *Who's Who* no longer includes information about either her school or her university.

country day schools which two per cent of American children attend.[33] And 61 per cent of its students came from the public schools (state schools) and parochial (Catholic) schools which 98 per cent of American students attend. At Yale some ten per cent of students were children of alumni, no doubt one of the reasons why alumni support American universities more generously than their counterparts in England.[34] At the same time, British politicians normally misunderstood both the nature and source of the ability of leading American universities and colleges to provide student support. Thus Laura Spence did not get from Harvard what the Brits think of as a scholarship; she got an aid package consisting of grant, loan and work. In so far as there are grants or scholarships, at most US independent colleges and universities, they come as much from the Robin Hood principle – charging the wealthy high fees partly to support a wide socio-economic range of students – as they do from the endowments.[35]

---

33. Statistics supplied by the Yale Admission Office. The American prep schools nevertheless suffered in the same way English public schools did. In 1950, Harvard admitted 69 of the 74 applicants from Andover. In 2000, it was 18 out of 89. In 1960, private schools represented 44 per cent of Harvard admissions; in 2000 it was 32 per cent. 'To Impress Colleges, Some Prep Schools Use Aggressive New Tactics', *Wall Street Journal*, 23 January 2001.

34. For an articulate statement about why Oxford gives no weight to alumni children or alumni gifts, see article by President of Trinity College, Oxford (Michael Beloff QC), 'Why money cannot – and should not – buy a place at Oxford', *The Times*, 20 December 2001. For scepticism about Trinity's 'patent virtue', see 'Third Time Lucky', *Oxford Magazine*, noughth week, Trinity Term 2002, p.1. Unfortunately, later in 2002, the Chaplain of Pembroke apparently attempted to sell a place to an undercover journalist from the *Sunday Times*. 'Oxford's begging bowl', *Sunday Times*, 24 March 2002; 'Revealed: Degrees for sale at Oxford', *id*; 'Drooping spires' *Economist*, 30 March 2002; 'Oxford fellows resign after bribery claim', *Guardian*, 25 March 2002. The scandal led to more rigorous control over college admissions. For a criticism of Oxford's old members' failure to support the university, see Felipe Fernández-Armesto, 'Decline and fall', *Spectator*, 29 December 2001. For an interesting analysis of the contrasting approaches of Oxford, Harvard and Princeton, with respect to fund raising and alumni preference in admissions, see Rachel Johnson, 'It's time for alumni preference', *Spectator*, 1 February 2003, p.13.

35. On 8 May 2001, *USA Today* reported the endowments as Harvard $18.846 billion, Yale $10.086 billion, Texas system $10.016 billion, Stanford $8.656 billion, Princeton $8.406 billion, MIT $6.486 billion, University of California system $5.646 billion.

The saga of the US-UK university interaction was on-going. Neil Rudenstein, the President of Harvard and former Provost of Princeton, observed at a seminar that the elite British institutions were in 'consistent and persistent deterioration because of inadequate funding. If you look at Oxbridge, it's a disaster, a nightmare... At Cambridge they haven't made a discovery since Watson and Crick discovered DNA back in the 1950's.'[36] The press picked up the inaugural lecture by David Cannadine, returning from Columbia University to London University, and observations about the absence of Nobel Prize winners at Oxford.[37] A series of articles by Alan Ryan, the political scientist returning from Princeton to Oxford, struck a similar theme.[38]

Princeton enhanced the frame in a different way. Oxford and Princeton developed a science relationship which Oxford announced as a partnership,[39] while Princeton appeared to look at it as a 'foothold in Europe'. Meanwhile the former President of Princeton, William Bowen, delivered the Romanes Lecture at Oxford, reminding Oxford what the Ivy League stood for, as once the older English universities had:

> *One of my greatest concerns is that, either inadvertently or by design, universities will be so bemused by market opportunities*

36. 'Oxford bristles at Harvard slur', *Sunday Times*, 15 July 2001. See also Letters to the Editor, *The Times*, 20 July 2001.

37. John Clare, 'The nightmares that trouble the sleep of the dreaming spires', *Daily Telegraph*, 18 August 1999; 'Oxford set to drop out of world league', *Financial Times*, 28 March 1998. The observation allegedly sent 'shivers of embarrassment up and down high tables'. 'Everyone knows Britain's best universities are world beaters. So why are they being outclassed by the Americans?', *Sunday Times*, 29 March 1998.

38. E.g. *Prospect*, September 1999.

39. 'Oxford teams up with Princeton', *Oxford Mail*, 22 November 2000; David Holmes, 'Has Oxford missed the boat?' *The Times*, 30 November 2000.

> *that they will lose sight of, or downplay, their most essential pur-*
> *poses. These include educating students broadly so that they may*
> *lead productive lives in a civilized society; serving as engines of*
> *opportunity and social mobility; creating new knowledge of every*
> *kind, including work that either has no immediate market value*
> *or may even threaten some commercial end; encouraging and pro-*
> *tecting the thoughtful critic and the dissenting voice; and defend-*
> *ing cultural, moral or intellectual values that no one can 'price'*
> *very well.*[40]

Bowen's 'essential purposes' of a university education were rather a long way from the 'insights' of the Dearing Report.

Chris Woodhead, the outspoken Chief Inspector of Schools, questioned the goal of fifty per cent of students in the tertiary sec-

---

40.   William G. Bowen, 'At a Slight Angle to the Universe: The University in a Digitized, Commercialized Age', Romanes Lecture, Oxford, 2000.

    A more domestic attack came from John Kay, brought in to run Oxford's new Said Business School. He obviously found that deanship frustrating. First of all the Oxford system of democracy made it difficult to accept the Said gift and then the difficulties of making decisions – and the universities' fixed salary scales – prevented the School from offering competitive salaries. See John Kay, 'A Lost Cause', *Prospect*, December 2000, p. 22. For the answers, see David Holmes, 'Oxford knows its own Business', *Times Higher Education Supplement*, 1 December 2000; Richard Morrison, 'Has Oxford missed the boat?', *The Times*, 30 November 2000; John Kay, 'So we agree not to agree?', *Times Higher Education Supplement*, 30 November 2000; 'Hopwood lashes out at "bitter" Kay', *Evening Standard*, 24 November 2000; 'Oxford University risks slipping into mediocrity', *Daily Telegraph*, 20 November 2000. The only time I attended Congregation (the democratic body of 3,000 dons who have the final say over all matters) was on the debate on the Said gift. It certainly was a remarkable discussion, where a group of obscurantist moral philosophers discussed the dangers resulting from the fact that one member of the Said Foundation might be involved in final academic decisions. There were fears that the position might be sold on the New York Stock Exchange! The moral philosophers felt they could never teach at a university where final decisions on academic appointments were made by a board which included non-academics. Since most of the speakers also had appointments at US universities (the way many Oxford academics deal with their risible salaries) and virtually all US universities have lay boards, the arguments had the air of the ludicrous. The debate, however, nearly lost Oxford the largest gift it had ever received and certainly deterred other major donors.

tor;[41] and he was soon followed by many others. Oxford discovered that, with the abolition of the college fee, the university rather than the colleges now called the shots[42] – something the bureaucrats in the DfEE had always wanted. Oxford continued to attempt to recruit students from the state sector[43] and was increasingly accused of naked discrimination against students from the independent sector.[44] Indeed, the Liberal Democrat MP for one of the Oxford constituencies boasted that 'for the first time Oxford University is positively discriminating in favour of students from comprehensive schools'.[45] As the election approached in the spring of 2001, the Conservatives announced that they were planning 'massive' one-off injections of capital so universities 'will be free to run their own financial affairs'. Being England, of course, there was a catch: they were not to be allowed to charge market fees.[46] It made no difference. The Conservatives were trashed in the election, eventually held in June 2001. There was another massive Labour landslide. Labour's contribution to the debate was to promise no top-up fees in the new Parliament and a new look at the funding of higher education. Such a new look was almost inevitable after devolution. The different parts of Britain seemed to be competing with one another: both Scotland and Wales were developing new funding mecha-

---

41. 'Woodhead warns on expansion', *Times Higher Education Supplement*, 15 September 2000, p. 5.

42. David Palfreyman, 'The Piper Calls the Tune', *Oxford Magazine*, Michaelmas term (2000), eighth week, p. 9. The change also emphasised the difference between the rich and the poor colleges. 'Wealthiest Oxford Colleges "offer better education"', *Daily Telegraph*, 26 April 2002.

43. 'Heads try to dispel Oxbridge myths', *The Times*, 2 April 2001.

44. 'You're too posh for the dreaming spires', *Sunday Times*, 4 February 2001.

45. Evan Harris, 'Higher Education: A Question of Access' in Prickett and Erskine-Hill (eds.), *op. cit.*, p. 42.

46. Press release, Conservative Central Office, 24 January 2001.

nisms. Labour responded by confirming, at the Brighton Party Conference in 2001, a goal of fifty per cent of the age cohort in higher education by 2010. There was still no greater clarity about what was meant by higher education. Was there any room for the idea of the univeristy as a place to learn to think and to absorb cultural values, with a view to training for leadership or was higher education's sole purpose now the credentialing of its clients and the enhancing of the economy?

9. *The Second Coming of New Labour and the Delayed Coming of the White Paper*

From the time of the general election in the summer of 2001 to the autumn of 2003, politics appeared as a repeat of the previous four years. In 2001, New Labour actually had more support from the press than in 1997.[1] The Conservatives, under William Hague, were humiliated, and under their cumbersome new leadership election machinery, they proceeded to elect the undistinguished Iain Duncan Smith (known as IDS; the staid *Economist* noted the initials also stood for 'In Deep Shit'). The Opposition, therefore, looked like the mob of Napoleon's army returning from Moscow in 1812/13, disorganised and dispirited, uttering dated mantras about the awfulness of the euro and the wonders of hunting. Even the Liberals, normally the custodian of *tot homines, quot sententiae*, appropriate for a party which had been out of power for nearly a hundred years, seemed a more serious opposition than the Conservatives.

---

1.   Margaret Scammill and Martin Harrop, 'The Press Disarmed' in David Butler and Dennis Kavanagh, *The British General Election of 2001*, (Basingstoke, 2001), p. 156.

The Labour Party's facade of New Labour was beginning to crack, as one would expect of a party with a 180 majority over all other parties (although with only forty-two per cent of the popular vote). Labour now had as much middle-class support as the Conservatives which, as they say in *1066 and All That*, was 'a Good Thing', since the working class (as the blue-collar vote used to be called), the traditional base of Labour support, was now in a minority. Yet the changing nature of the voting support in some ways emphasised the differences between Old Labour and the modernisers; particularly as the modernisers' rivalries deepened and their leaders fought for the support of traditional Labour voters.

Nowhere was this clearer than in the friction between Tony Blair and Gordon Brown. They had been friends; they were both modernisers. Surprisingly, in a nation that has largely abandoned God, they were both Christians. In opposition, both realised that the old mantra of 'tax and spend' would not propel Labour back into power. There, however, the similarity ended. Blair was an Anglicised Scot, an English barrister, Oxford educated and an ardent Christian at the Anglo-Catholic end of the spectrum. Brown was the son of a Presbyterian minister and a dour anti-social Scot; he was devoid of Blair's articulate style, but had far better roots into Old Labour. Indeed, Brown's control over the Scottish Labour party, overrepresented in Westminster for historical reasons, was remarkable. As the years went by, the instinctive liberal values of Tony Blair came increasingly into conflict with the Old Labour tribal views more frequently represented by the introspective Brown.

It was into this cauldron that the issue of higher education was thrown. As we have seen, by the beginning of Labour's second term, all of higher education, from the further education colleges, through the new universities to the old traditional academic universities, was grossly underfunded.[2] In a report to the Treasury, Sir Gareth Roberts called for a massive investment in research.[3] It was, however, the old universities that had attracted much of the attention. The Conservatives, without much thought, had abolished the independence of universities in 1988, and then homogenised universities in 1992. When New Labour came to power in 1997, it made illegal the one thing which might have restored the universities' independence and allowed academic universities the ability to compete internationally – the right to charge fees. Having been put on the homogenisation path by the Conservatives, the elite universities had been increasingly frozen into that pattern by New Labour. It looked as if the English universities were to follow the French and German universities, which have been in decline for the previous thirty years as they have struggled with declining government funding and effectively open admissions. (The French solution was to cull a significant number of students at the end of the first year.) Moreover English universities did not have the compensation that Germany – at least for research – had in the Max Planck Institutes (although research funds in England were directed primarily to the elite universities) nor for training an intellectual elite that the *Hautes Écoles* provided in France.[4] It was Tony Blair's sudden interest – probably stimulated by Roy Jenkins – in

---

2.   'Our universities are tatty, the staff-student ratios have gone to hell, academics are paid a pittance. You can't have university funding at the rate it has been and remain internationally competitive', Peter Lampl, *Sunday Times*, 12 January 2003.

3.   'Roberts calls for science rethink', *Times Higher Education Supplement*, 8 March 2002. And see HM Treasury, *Investing in Innovation: A Strategy for Science, Engineering and Technology*, July 2002.

4.   At times Margaret Hodge appeared to be proposing a similar solution for the UK: 'Britain needs more graduates in a mass higher education system, but we need to maintain a cohort of the most highly achieving graduates who will fuel our future growth and prosperity'. Cited by Frances Beckett, 'How businesses will pay the university piper', *New Statesman*, 20 January 2003.

seeing the universities strive for independence and excellence that was most threatening to his backbenchers.[5]

As the underfunding of higher education and the declining possibility of English universities competing with the leading North American universities slowly became plain, the tone of parliamentary debates changed. During the nineties, debates on higher education had been characterised by Roy Jenkins announcing that of the five great universities in the world, two were in England. (No prizes for naming them.) When the House of Lords debated higher education in November 2002, the mood was much more sombre. The plight of all universities was accepted. The inadequate support of universities was admitted, as were the difficulties of further education colleges, the 'sharp end' of access, whose salary scales had fallen behind those of secondary schools. At thirty, university lecturers were earning less than MPs' secretaries and less than secondary school teachers.[6] As Lord Renfrew put it: 'Britain's world-class universities and Britain's other universities have fallen into deficit through what has become a bankrupting funding policy...that is beginning to lead to irreversible decline.'[7] Lord Baker – the author of so many of the universities' misfortunes – announced: 'The real trouble is that Gordon Brown treats universities as a nationalized industry – almost the last of our nationalized industries. They are underfunded, over controlled and bullied.'[8]

---

5.   In October 2002, he told MPs: 'There is an issue of freedom for universities and about how we ensure the British universities remain in the top 10 universities in the world.' Cited in 'Will top-up fees be the issue that finally divides Blair and Brown?', *Daily Telegraph*, 21 January 2003.

6.   And dramatically less than teachers in the best public schools. 'Eton's assets fall by £53m', *Daily Telegraph*, 24 July 2002.

7.   *Parl. Deb.*, House of Lords, vol. 641, cols 789–90 (27 November 2002).

8.   *Ibid*, col. 757.

Outside the Chamber, he claimed: 'Year by year our universities decline: facilities become shabbier; classes grow larger; research equipment is not updated quickly; libraries are underfunded; and good academics, whose salaries have fallen 40 per cent relative to other salaries, move overseas.'[9]

Lord Smith of Clifton, a Liberal Democrat peer and former Vice-Chancellor of the University of Ulster, made it clear that 'the UK now lacks any multi-faculty university that can claim to be on a par with those of the Ivy League in the United States'.[10] Outside the House, Baroness Williams, leader of the Liberal Democrats in the Lords, (an undistinguished Higher Education Minister under Wilson and an undistinguished Secretary of Education under Callaghan and for many years a professor at the Kennedy School of Government at Harvard), admitted that 'underfunding now seriously affects both the quality of research and teaching. At the bottom end there is a trail of colleges and universities which are not even second-rate. And at the top end, I doubt whether there are any internationally first-rate universities left in Britain; perhaps a few departments here and there'. To the Baroness, the solution was not top-up fees but more taxes and presumably funding linked to the quality of the institution, although she carefully avoided saying this. The position was odd bearing in mind that the intellectual clout for top-up fees came from her predecessor as leader of the Liberal Democrats in the Lords, Roy Jenkins. The Liberal Democrats were no more attracted to the independence of the uni-

---

9. Kenneth Baker, 'Top-up fees will let universities walk tall', *Daily Telegraph*, 27 November 2002.

10. *Parl. Deb.*, House of Lords, vol. 641, col. 761. He added, 'There are, of course, specialist institutions, such as Imperial College and the London School of Economics, that contain a large measure of international excellence, and many universities have so far managed to maintain varying amounts of research activity that can compete with the best in the world.'

versity sector than were the other parties;[11] indeed less so. In an effort to position themselves to the left of New Labour and at the same time to appeal to the self-interest of the English middle class, it is arguable that the Liberal Democrat position represented party politics at its cleverest or its worst.

Lord Baker noted that during the previous five years, no Nobel Prize had gone to persons teaching in an English university. That was a dramatic change of attitude in only five years.[12] Many Conservatives thought the best solution would be top-up fees – essentially what all American universities have. As Lord Baker pointed out, although universities vilified Mrs Thatcher for forcing them to make overseas students pay top-up fees, 'by that action she saved the financial position of most universities in this country'.[13] To Baker, the logic was irrefutable: 'So far as the government are concerned, top-up fees start at Kuala Lumpur. So parents in Kuala Lumpur can pay top-up fees whereas parents from Kidderminster cannot. That presents an ethical and interesting position for the Government because if top-up fees are discriminatory, harsh, and disruptive of social harmony, those effects would be felt in Kuala Lumpur, just as they would in Kidderminster.'[14] Support for top-up fees came generally from the right, and from cross-bench peers (for example, Lord Butler, a former

---

11.   'Roundtable: University Challenge', *Prospect,* January 2003, p. 20. The more intelligent Liberal Democrat peers – Lord Goodhart, Lord Smith of Clifton and Lord Wallace of Saltaire – realize that some form of fees must come.

12.   In a speech at George Washington University on 24 March 1997, the author pointed out that Oxford had no Nobel Prize winners on the faculty and that it was holding on to its international reputation 'by its fingertips'. Robert Stevens, *Barbarians at the Gate* (George Washington University, 1998). Some paranoid members of the Oxford establishment believed that the date of the lecture (certainly not decided by me) was designed to undercut the Oxford spring alumni meeting!

13.   *Parl. Deb.*, House of Lords, vol. 641, col. 554 (27 November 2002).

14.   *Ibid*, col. 755.

Head of the Civil Service and by then Master of University College, Oxford) but also from some members of the left. Lord Desai, an Anglo-Indian Labour peer and Professor of Economics at the LSE (most of whose students are fee-paying overseas students),[15] argued: 'For 35 years I have heard the same argument: if we charge anything, the poor will not get access. The middle class are clever; they always use the poor to justify their own subsidies.'[16]

While some Liberal Democrat peers supported top-up fees, Labour peers in general did not. Lord Morgan, formerly the Vice-Chancellor of Aberystwyth, did not believe that bursaries would result from top-up fees in the way predicted by Lord Butler.[17] Lord Davies of Coity was more doctrinaire: 'Never must a price tag be the factor that determines who does and who does not go to university and must not determine which university anyone goes to…Our children go to primary and secondary schools and they make no payment. So why should we then introduce further charges for the provision of higher education?'[18] Top-up fees were of course opposed by the universities' UK mouthpiece, Baroness Warwick, because they would lead to a 'two tier' system of universities.[19] The abolition of the binary line – to mix metaphors – had come home to roost.

The House of Lords debate took place amid the painful wait for the White Paper on the funding of higher education. The call for

15.   See Lord Wedderburn, (Emeritus professor at the LSE) noting that in 1978/9, the government provided sixty-four per cent of the LSE's income; in 1998/9, twenty-six per cent. *Ibid*, vol. 607, col. 1315.

16.   *Ibid*, cols. 787–8. 'We give everybody a subsidy, including the very rich middle classes. That is partly because we are too afraid to implement a proper means test which would benefit only the poor, and partly because fees are too low.'

17.   *Ibid*, col. 797.

18.   *Ibid*, col. 829.

19.   *Ibid*, col. 760.

the paper originated from the Millbank machine, New Labour's emulation of the Clinton campaign machine. In focus groups, Millbank discovered that the most unpopular act of the first New Labour government had been the imposition of the university fee. (This was particularly true for middle-class voters and students. Whereas in the old universities students were greatly agitated by the fee,[20] in the new universities, where there were fewer affluent middle-class students whose parents had to pay, the fee was far less of an issue.) Then, as the 2001 election approached, the party promised first that there would be no top-up fees in its second administration and second, that there would be a White Paper on the future financing of higher education.

The White Paper, which had originally been promised for late in 2001, was, however, constantly delayed. There were various reasons for this. First, the Education Secretary for the first year of the new administration was Estelle Morris, a sweet but ineffective former comprehensive school teacher, with little understanding of, or interest in, universities.[21] The Higher Education Minister, Margaret Hodge – a child of Jewish immigrants, a former member of the loony left (as leader of Labour in Islington Council, she flew the Red Flag over the Town Hall)[22] transformed into a member of New Labour – was more effective. She was, however, faced with an intractable problem: she wanted England to retain serious international universities but also wanted to raise the standards of all universities. As she put it, she wanted both excellence and equality. With the English system of

---

20.   Led at Oxford by the Foreign Secretary's son. *The Times*, 5 December 2002.

21.   Daughter of a Labour Minister, she had gone to a teacher training college in Coventry, associated with the University of Warwick.

22.   When, in the spring reshuffle of 2003, she was made Minister for Children, the past at Islington came to haunt her, particularly the mismanaged social services. 'Sex abuse scandal: Minister accused', *Evening Standard*, 30 June 2003.

funding, that was unlikely to be possible.[23] While everyone by then agreed that the university system was on the point of collapse, the way forward became subject to a significant split in the Labour Party. The delay in the publication of the White Paper was aggravated by the ambivalence of the universities. In general the older universities were in favour of top-up fees, but this view was not shared even by some of the Russell Group and Regent House (the Cambridge equivalent of Congregation at Oxford) had doubts.[24] At the same time most, but not all, of the new universities were opposed (although some vice-chancellors, including the Vice-Chancellor of the University of Central England, were in favour). Opponents sensed that fees would mean differential fees; and differential fees would mean a formalised hierarchy of universities. To this Lord Desai, the Labour peer, answered: 'What is happening now is that by charging a single price we have to ration. Such rationing results in bad education ... Who gets such bad education? People from lower income classes and ethnic minorities. They go to ghastly universities.'[25] While the old universities were seeking to regain the independence they had had under the UGC, the new universities, which had never had either the independence or the resources associated with it, were understandably less agitated. The war cry against fees was once more the middle-class one that the poor would be unable to attend universities,[26] although the increasing evi-

---

23. 'Never mind the quality, feel the quantity', *Guardian*, 20 May 2002.

24. 'Top-up fees would hit poorer students, Cambridge warns', *Guardian*, 15 November 2002; 'Cambridge rejects top-up fees as row over funding splits elite universities', *Evening Standard*, 14 November 2002.

25. *Parl. Deb.*, House of Lords, vol. 641, col. 788 (27 November 2002).

26. Lord Desai had a rather vigorous response to that: 'I believe we should make everyone pay the going rate – I would prefer an income-contingent loan system – and then take our entire current budget which is used for tuition fees and put it into a fund for bursaries. There should be zero subsidies. We could finance up to one-third of our students with full bursaries if one stopped the indiscriminate giving of subsidies to the undeserving middle classes.' *Ibid*, col. 788.

dence was that it was the absence of maintenance grants rather than fees – which were anyway means tested – that was discouraging the poor from attending university. Another point was rarely made. There was often little push to get students from poorer families into universities[27] due to the frequent, but by no means universal, lack of parental interest in academic subjects in social classes IV and V, the weakness in state education especially in the inner cities, and the prevailing yob culture. Politicians, however, dare not admit the possibility of an absence of push, any more than they were willing to admit to defects in the state system of secondary education. New Labour assumed that the failure to recruit from the economically and socially disadvantaged was the result of an absence of pull on the part of the universities.

The ambivalence of universities about how they should be funded in the future made the public's view further confused. There were complex political currents flowing. Sir Richard Sykes, Rector of Imperial College, pointed out the absurdity of university funding in the spring of 2002;[28] he talked of fees of £10,500 or, in order to provide bursaries on the Robin Hood principle, £15,000.[29] It became known that Tony Blair had been converted to top-up fees, both by his sometime mentor Roy Jenkins and by his policy adviser in No. 10, Andrew Adonis. Both were anathema to

---

27.   Of children who obtain five passes at A B or C in GCSE only one-fifth have parents who are unskilled manual workers; two-thirds have parents whose occupations are professional or managerial. Anthony Smith, *Education, Education, Education*, p. 33. On a related issue, only some 33 per cent of white boys get A–C GCSEs (compared with nearly 40 per cent of Indian and only 12 per cent of Afro-Caribbean). 'Taking the rap', *Economist*, 11 January 2003.

28.   'Elite Universities', *Financial Times*, 28 May 2002.

29.   'Imperial College to raise fees from £1,100 to £10,500', *Independent*, 18 October 2002. For a scathing view of the funding of higher education by a businessman VC, see Vincent Watts (Vice-Chancellor of the University of East Anglia), 'How to go bankrupt very slowly', *Financial Times*, 18 May 2001. On the Sykes proposal see 'Reform of universities urged to aid science', *Financial Times*, 27 May 2002. Academics were chiefly fascinated by Sykes's pension from a pharmaceutical company of £700,000 p.a.

Labour backbenchers; Adonis was an Oxford intellectual who represented all they hated in New Labour, Jenkins the Chancellor of Oxford who had split the Labour Party in the early eighties with the establishment of the Social Democratic Party. It became known that the Prime Minister had held a 'secret' meeting with Vice-Chancellors who supported a top-up fee.[30] In no time, some 180 backbenchers had signed a motion opposed to top-up fees, which would, they argued, keep the poor out of universities, establish a two-tier university system and encourage elitism. The catchphrases were predictable. It was a classic case of Old Labour's commitment to equality of outcome rather than equality of opportunity. Such views, however, were supported by a series of articles in the *New Statesman* and by columns in the *Observer* pointing out the dangers of meritocracy, which inevitably led to inequality.[31] It was all strangely inconsistent with the enterprise economy, espoused by New Labour and used by them as a reason for not touching the public schools – which were educational charities just like the old universities. Indeed, New Labour, as old Tory, had a touching faith in businessmen and felt that if only universities linked up with them, the latter's problems would be solved.[32]

If Andrew Adonis was anathema to the 'old' Labour types on the back benches, Lord Jenkins was hated by Gordon Brown, who

---

30 'Secret Blair bid to boost top-up cause', *Times Higher Education Supplement*, 22 November 2002. Apparently this included the Vice-Chancellors of Oxford, Cambridge, Warwick, Bristol, Nottingham, University of Central England, Imperial College and Sussex.

31 For a sense of the genre, see Will Hutton, *The State We're In*, (London, 1996), ch. 7 ('Why Inequality Doesn't Work'); 'The hypocrisy of going private', *Observer*, 23 March 2003.

32. Margaret Hodge enthused over the University of Warwick: 'They are already perusing the route encouraged by Bill Gates.' Frances Beckett, 'How business will pay the University piper', *New Statesman*, 20 January, 2003, p. 28. See also the Report from the Department of Trade and Industry, the Treasury and the Department of Education and Skills, *Investing in Innovation: A Strategy for Science, Engineering and Technology*, 2002.

could take hatred to a fine art. After all, Jenkins was not only a deserter from the Labour ship but an adviser to his rival, Tony Blair. Also, at the time of the Laura Spence affair, Jenkins, the Chancellor of Oxford, had pointed out that there were more Etonians at the University of Edinburgh, Brown's university, than there were at Oxford. (Denis Healey, at the time of the Labour leadership election in 1976, had famously remarked that Roy Jenkins was 'ill-suited to the politics of class and ideology which played so large a role in the Labour Party'.[33]) Moreover, Brown, in his effort to replace Blair as Prime Minister, needed the old-line Labour backbenchers. He first of all leaked that he could not support allowing universities to charge fees because universities were too badly run to handle the money. (It is always fascinating to see how each British administration comes in announcing the end of centralisation and immediately give reasons for strengthening central control.)[34] The money would have to be controlled centrally. Very soon, however, it was leaked that he also opposed fees because they would lead to a two-tier system of universities, elitism and the exclusion of the poor.[35] The issue inevitably became tied up with the issue of public services generally. To win the support of the unions, Brown had poured money into public services, without requiring the kind of reforms among employees necessary to make the system work effectively. The Blairites sought to revive the pub-

---

33. Naughtie, *op. cit.*, p. 202.

34. Labour was also talking of taking power from local authorities with respect to planning and the police.

35. Brown's 'deeply felt egalitarian instincts, a not unjustified reaction to the rigidities of Britain's historically rigid class system, led him to support policies that at best will provide citizens with equal, but mediocre, healthcare and education'. Irwin Seltzer, 'Brown is winning even though he's wrong', *The Times*, 20 February 2003. Brown, an advocate of the enterprise economy, drew the line at education and health. 'Warning by Brown on market role', *Guardian*, 4 February 2003.

lic services by using private contractors where necessary and allowing certain providers to opt out of central control. Brown was outraged, although he allowed 'Dobbo' (Frank Dobson – not the sharpest pencil in the Labour box) to run the campaign against foundation hospitals – NHS hospitals which were to be beacons of a more open system – and top-up fees.[36]

It was not that Brown was opposed to giving more money to higher education. He, however, supported a graduate tax, whereby those with degrees would pay more by way of income tax. This would both make the tax system more progressive and give him control over the universities. As with everything else, there were various possible versions of such a graduate tax. All, however, had three problems: that the money would not come in for some while, that universities would have no real independence and (a problem only for some) that it would be impossible to distinguish among universities. There were also political problems at least selling the tax to the middle-class supporters of New Labour. It would mean, for instance, that, using the assumption of an additional three per cent on income tax, over twenty-five years, a person joining a leading international law firm in the City could pay an additional £1.5 million in tax over those years. The government would also have to borrow at least an additional £3 billion before money started coming in. Other difficulties included how to tax the ever-increasing number of EU students attending UK universities – especially from Germany where universities had increasingly given up on teaching. (So had the French universities, but French students share their nation's chauvinism.) Moreover, many UK graduates move abroad to work, while the

---

36. 'Backbench attack on top-up fees and hospital shake-up', *Financial Times*, 15 November 2002.

English landed gentry run their estates through companies; assuming there was a fiscal threshold for repayment, the young from this group might never repay. Others questioned whether it was fair for those women who married rather than worked, to be freed from all obligation to pay.[37]

37.   This whole debate raises some important issues over the UK approach to taxation and rights under the Welfare State.

  Unlike the US, taxation in the UK is based not on nationality, but on residence. Moreover the UK system is more formalistic than US tax law; and residence is more generously construed – towards the taxpayer – than it is in US law. The result is that the fourteen million UK citizens who live abroad (up from seven million in 1980) pay no tax although, if registered, they may vote in UK elections. Moreover, they enjoy UK titles. Tax exiles such as Sir Sean Connery (knighted apparently for his support for independence for Scotland) and Sir Mick Jagger pay no tax. (Indeed, Mick Jagger has yet to collect his knighthood from the Queen for fear of staying too long in England for tax purposes.)

  Britain also has more generous definitions of domicile and residence. If someone is able to prove that he is neither domiciled nor resident in the UK, no tax is payable. Many wealthy Asians, Middle Easterners and Americans have houses – sometimes multiple houses – in the UK and providing they do not stay more than three months in any one year, they are free to do this without paying tax. Such largesse explains the buoyancy at the top end of the property market in the UK. British people are able to achieve comparable gains if they are able to establish a claim to residence in one of the British tax havens in the West Indies or closer to home in the Isle of Man or the Channel Islands, which conveniently also have opaque banking laws and a low flat tax rate. Residence within the UK normally still only makes the person liable for money arising outside the UK if they are also domiciled in the UK. Thus resident American merchant bankers claiming domicile in the US can keep their money off-shore and only pay it when they remit it to the UK. In fact, this arrangement is of less importance to Americans, who are taxed by the US government on the basis of nationality, irrespective of residence. It is, however, a great convenience to Middle Eastern arms dealers, Swedish businessmen and Greek ship owners. Brits working abroad have similar benefits and help in Britain's invisible exports.

  Even for UK citizens who are both resident and domiciled, they too may sometimes avoid UK tax by establishing a trust outside the UK. When Gordon Brown appointed Geoffrey Robinson Comptroller-General to sort out these problems, it emerged he had a large off-shore trust! See Tom Bower, *The Paymaster: Geoffrey Robinson, Maxwell and New Labour* (London, 2001), pp. 87–8.

  These problems lap over to the Welfare State. There are, for instance, more than 500,000 Brits living on the Costa del Sol in Spain, bringing the cultural benefits of Britain to the 'backward' Spanish. Even more have retired to France and Italy, and as in Spain, they appear to pay neither local nor UK tax. In 2000, 300,000 Brits emigrated; 'The pull of Provence', *Economist*, 26 April 2003. Whatever the technical rules, they nevertheless expect to be able to use British public services – including the National Health Services and universities. Even as EU residents their children are able to go to Newcastle or Exeter either free or for the minimal fee. If

The Chancellor of the Exchequer, in an outburst in the *Guardian* office,[38] claimed that the Prime Minster's plan for top-up fees was 'madness'. He was supported in this by David Blunkett – one of his rivals to succeed Tony Blair – and then left-wingers in the Cabinet like Clare Short[39] and Helen Liddell. Only Tony Blair seemed committed to top-up fees.[40] At this point the overall position of the Prime Minister was weakened when his wife, Cherie Booth, a successful lawyer, unwisely used her lifestyle guru (Cherie's New Age tendencies are more Santa Cruz than Downing Street) helped by the latter's boyfriend (not only an Australian but also a con-man) to buy two flats for their son. The daily papers, which, in the absence of a serious opposition have increasingly taken over the role of opposition, mercilessly, and probably unfairly, attacked the Prime Minister and his wife. As the attack dragged on – and the Brown wing of the Cabinet also failed to share the Blair enthusiasm for George Bush and Donald Rumsfeld's attack on Iraq – No. 10 seemed to be backing away from top-up fees. The irony was that fees, carefully means tested, would be the fairest and least regressive solution. Fees and means testing, however, were anathema to the Labour left and an outrage to the middle classes, accustomed to their university fee freebie. Thus Labour, for political and electoral

---

the families now live in the US or Australia, an accommodation address or a grandparent can transfer the cost of university education to some local authority. For the very wealthy Middle Eastern or Far Eastern students, four years for their children at an English public school may establish residence for subsidized university fees (if not for taxes) and means the British taxpayer not only provides the cost of university education but also provides interest-free loans – which frequently have to be collected from a distant or even non-existent address.

38. 'Brown attacks Blair's "ridiculous" top-up fees', *Mail on Sunday*, 1 December 2002. Brown was supported by Clare Short, who saw herself as Brown's deputy in a new administration.

39. She described top-up fees as a 'really bad idea'. 'The cost of learning', *Daily Telegraph*, 19 November 2002.

40. 'Blair tells party to accept public service diversity', *Financial Times*, 10 December 2002.

reasons, were pushed into solutions more regressive and less attractive to lower socio-economic groups.[41]

By this time, however, there had been rather dramatic political changes. Estelle Morris, battered by some odd behaviour by the examining boards for A levels was, rather unfairly, held responsible for the chaos. When it was clear that she was about to be pig-in-the-middle in a battle between Brown and Blair on university fees she threw in the towel.[42] In a most unpolitician-like way, in the autumn of 2002, she admitted that she was not up to the job. She was rapidly replaced by Charles Clarke, then Chairman of the Labour Party, and a Blairite. Clarke, Cambridge educated (maths and economics), the son of a civil servant who had been regarded as a bruiser, replicated his father's reputation.[43] The son had been a self-proclaimed Marxist President of the National Union of Students in 1976, when he famously opined: 'Fundamental economic change ... will relegate capitalism to the history books where it belongs.' He was also a bruiser in appearance, replicating my commitment to exercise, diet and abstinence. He, however, was a clever politician, although hated by the Chancellor for having publicly regretted that there had not been a vote on Blair and Brown for leader at the death of John Smith. Clarke had been satisfied that Brown would have been clearly defeated. The Chancellor did not easily forgive such sentiments.

Clarke cleverly wove a path between the warring Labour leaders.[44] He announced that instinctively he was opposed to top-up

41.   For a variation on this, see Sir John Kingman, former Vice-Chancellor of Bristol, 'The new university challenge', *Daily Telegraph*, 1 August 2001.

42.   'Student fees row was "last straw" for Morris', *Independent on Sunday*, 27 October 2002.

43.   Rachel Sylvester, 'Pay attention at the back: Bruiser's in charge and there will be questions', *Daily Telegraph*, 14 December 2002.

44.   'The stealthy elitist', *Economist*, 21 December 2002. Clarke said he was not opposed to elites, he just wanted to ensure talent had access to them. 'Education Secretary backs elites', *Financial Times*, 20 November 2002.

fees, while making it clear that the rescue package to save the impoverished universities would not come mainly from the Treasury. He rapidly accepted Tony Blair's political statement,[45] in capitulating to the Brown wing, that parents would not have to spend large sums up front.[46] To placate the Brownites still further, he made noises about abolishing the last 160 grammar schools, just as the *Economist* was arguing that the abolition of the bulk of the grammar schools had made England a more class-riven society.[47] For the first time for decades, however, England did seem to have an Education Secretary who was prepared to think about some of the fundamental issues. Indeed, if it were not a term of abuse in England, he might have been described as an intellectual. He later threw this characterisation of himself into doubt by announcing that 'education for its own sake ... was a bit dodgy', singling out classics and medieval history 'I don't mind there being some medievalists around for ornamental purposes, but there is no reason for this state to pay for them.' He later added that what he really objected to was the medieval notion of a community of scholars and that the state should only pay for subjects of 'clear usefulness'.[48] The Secretary had adopted the now fashionable view that universities existed primarily to prime the economic pump.

Nevertheless the discussion paper he issued in November 2002 was an important step forward.[49] Unlike much of the earlier debate on high-

45.   See also 'Pass rate soars as pupils play the system', *Daily Telegraph*, 15 August 2002.

46.   For Tony Blair's capitulation on up-front fees, see 'Blair backtracks on top-up fees', *The Times*, 5 December 2002; 'Blair retreats on top-up fees', *Daily Telegraph*, 5 December 2002.

47.   'How Britain's elite has changed', *Economist*, 7 December 2002.

48.   'Clarke dismisses medieval historians', *Guardian*, 9 May 2003; 'Clarke lays into useless history', *Times Higher Education Supplement*, 9 May 2003.

49.   No Title, Department for Education and Skills, 20 November 2002.

er education, it showed a willingness to address the purpose of universities. First and foremost, he admitted that morale in higher education was poor, that the best universities were losing some of their top faculty members and that there was a massive need for capital investment. The paper was significant because it acknowledged bluntly that:

> *It is hopeless to pretend that all universities are the same or even similar, since they are manifestly not. This should be recognised, even celebrated ...Government should acknowledge this in the way universities are funded ... [and] should try and offer universities the opportunity to define their own mission and then carry that through with minimum central government interference ... Academic independence is a genuine value which should not be jeopardised ... [but] it is entirely reasonable for government to ask why the class intake to universities, despite expansion, still remains at 75 per cent from middle-class backgrounds, as it did forty years ago.*

In response to the question about funding, Clarke raised three issues. First, why did UK alumni not support their universities in the way US alumni do?[50] Second, Clarke asked why, if the young were happy to take out a loan for a car or a holiday and expected to be in debt most of their lives, they were reluctant to take out a loan for university education 'that lasts for life',[51] and brings another

---

50. One suspects the main reasons are not the tax system, which is now quite supportive of gifts, but the fact that universities have been part of the Welfare State for fifty years and there is an expectation they will be supported by the tax system. Moreover, under government pressure, children of alumni gain no advantage in the university admissions process. Public schools, which charge large fees and give an admissions break to the children of alumni, have been reasonably successful in raising money from their alumni.

51. Some two-thirds of UK 'families' (defining the term broadly) own their own homes. During both 2001 and 2002 the average price of houses increased by £20,000 in each year. Since the average price of a house in 2000 was some £100,000, it meant the average family in the UK had made a gain (not necessarily realised) of £40,000 in twenty-four months.

£400,000 of additional income?[52] Third, Clarke pointed out that
while the state put money into universities because of the benefits
they brought 'to society and the economy ... it should be clear that
dependence solely upon the general taxpayer is an approach which
will inevitably restrain university spending and inhibit the drive to
raise standards of both teaching and research'.

The new Secretary moved fast. He increased by twenty-five per
cent the amount going to further education colleges and sixth-form
colleges.[53] He enabled those institutions to compete with secondary
schools in salaries. The Brown groupies, however, remained determined to punish leading universities for having too few working-
class and state school students. Articles in the *New Statesman* suggested that universities should be forced to discriminate against
public-school students;[54] after all, only 'stuffy old dons' cared about

Family Spending, the government's survey of such matters, showed that between 1974
and 2000, while the percentage of income spent on housing had risen slightly (from 14 to 17
per cent), as had the amount spent on cars (from 11 to 14 per cent), the percentage spent on
food, fuel and power, non-alcoholic drinks, tobacco and clothing had dropped by about a third.
Still four per cent went on alcohol. The largest increases were in household services – mainly
telephones, including mobile telephones – which had risen from £2.80 (in 2000 prices) to
£17.30 per month. The biggest gainer was leisure services, primarily foreign holidays, which
tripled. In 2000–1 prices, these rose from £17 a week in 1974 to £51 a week in 2000. Stationery
Office, National Statistics, *Family Spending*, 2002. Surveys suggested that the fear of debt had
been overblown. 'University is worth the debt, say students', *The Times*, 6 December 2002.
Those that had a negative attitude to debt – allegedly the poorest groups – had an even more
negative attitude to higher education.

52.   Lord Norton of Louth, a professor at the University of Hull, has questioned whether
this figure is meaningful for some of the new universities. *Parl. Deb.*, House of Lords, vol. 641,
col. 828 (27 November 2002). The University of East London had been advertising on the
London Underground that graduates earned an additional £400,000. It may be this does not
apply in this particular university. On the other hand, the OECD reported that English graduates had the highest rate of return in the EU. 'UK graduates earn highest rate of return',
Times Higher Education Supplement, 30 August 2002.

53.   Department for Education and Skills, 'Record Investment in Return for Tough Reform
– Clarke', press release, 19 November 2002.

54.   Francis Burkett, 'Discriminate more, not less', *New Statesman*, 9 December 2002, p. 25;
Rachel Johnson, 'A bias against excellence', *Spectator*, 23 March 2002.

Brown's inaccuracies about Laura Spence. The middle classes defended their corner. The Chairman of the Headmasters' Conference threatened that they would bring a case about universities' discrimination against public schools under the Human Rights Act;[55] Clement Freud, grandson of the Great Man and a former Liberal MP, said the Court of Human Rights in Strasbourg would tell the public schools to 'fuck off'.[56] The private girls' schools insisted taxes should be raised rather than allowing universities to charge fees;[57] after all if universities charged fees the demand for private secondary education would fall. (Bear in mind that the leading English public schools charge tuition, room and board at the US Ivy League level – or above – and give far less financial aid – in a society where average incomes are two-thirds of those in the United States.[58]) The dynamic new Chairman of the Bar Council, the barristers' trade union, was horrified that top-up fees would prevent the poor coming to the bar; there was no mention of whether QCs, whose incomes now average some quarter of a million pounds a year, might be willing to pay fees for their children at university, thereby making bursaries for the poor feasible. He later announced his intention of using the new Human Rights Act to prevent the poor (and, of course, QCs' children) from having to pay fees.[59] The editor of the right-wing *Daily Telegraph* dis-

---

55. Lucy Hodges, 'Where rights come first', *Independent*: Higher Education, 14 November 2002.

56. Peterborough, *Daily Telegraph*, 8 November 2002.

57. 'Girls' Schools Association: Top-up fees are not the answer', *The Times*, 19 November 2002.

58. For the argument that the English public schools should emulate Andover, which spends thirty per cent of its income on need-based financial aid, see 'Who's paying Lord Snooty's fees?', *New Statesman*, 21 July 2003.

59. 'Legal battle alert over university funding', *The Times*, 27 January 2003.

covered that to have universities charge real fees would be another of Gordon Brown's stealth taxes.[60]

Behind the froth, more serious thinking was going on. Even the Murdoch papers thought the young were going to have to pay more,[61] while the *Economist* could not believe that Gordon Brown was as anti-intellectual, with respect to universities, as the attitudes attributed to him suggested.[62] The House of Commons Education and Skills Committee produced a useful report on student support,[63] rejecting the Scottish and Welsh solutions, but calling for far more generous maintenance support for poor students. For more affluent students the Committee had no problem expecting students to pay more and thought it inappropriate that they should receive interest-free loans. Rather courageously, the Committee argued that students should be educated about the value of going to university and the appropriateness of borrowing for university. They were attracted to the Crawford-Barr scheme of income contingent loans; something the *Financial Times* reported that Secretary Clarke was leaning towards as a means of bridging the Blair-Brown divide.

Meanwhile no one was denying the increasingly parlous state of the universities. The tutorial and even the small seminar were disappearing from the universities; this made it possible for more full-time students in universities to work during term time either out of

---

60. Charles Moore, Diary, *Spectator*, 13 July 2002.

61. 'Fairer student fees', Editorial, *Sunday Times*, 24 November 2002.

62. 'A technocrat like the Chancellor cannot plausibly subscribe to such an extreme form of egalitarianism that he would happily preside over the slow destruction of Britain's best universities, nor can someone who exults in the collective brain power of the Treasury deny there's a place for intellectual elitism.' Bagehot, *Economist*, 7 December 2002.

63. *Post-16 Student Support*, HC445, 11 July 2002. See also Education and Employment Committee, *Higher Education: Access*, HC205, 30 January 2001.

need or lifestyle choices.[64] Employers were complaining more frequently about the 'dumbing down' of degrees.[65] There were suggestions that appointments at English universities were increasingly mediocre.[66] The *Times Higher Education Supplement* reported
that 2,000 academic posts were to go during that academic year.[67]
King's College London talked of closing its famed chemistry
department.[68] Oxford made considerable cuts in staff as the deficit
deepened, and Oxford colleges discussed dramatic cutbacks in the
tutorial system.[69] There was more talk of charging real fees, even
at the risk of the government vetoing them.[70] The administrative
leadership of Oxford, only five years after the North Report had
ruled it out, warned that unless there were a serious top-up fee, it
might have to go independent.[71] Cambridge had a withering

---

64. Watson and Bowden, 'Can We Be Equal and Excellent Too?', p. 17. By 2003, the OUSU
claimed that one-fifth of Oxford undergraduates had part-time jobs during term-time,
although it is the policy of the University not to allow such activities. Nationally, the press
reported that half of university students had part-time jobs during term time.

65. 'Industry hits out at diluted degree trend', *Times Higher Education Supplement*, 4 April
2003.

66. Michael Burleigh, 'Few of you would get an interview here', *Times Higher Education
Supplement*, 4 April 2003.

67. See also 'Dons feel the chill', *Education Guardian*, 26 November 2002. For a more conservative figure see 'Cuts mean universities risk loss of 1400 jobs', *Guardian*, 21 May 2002.

68. 'Prestigious chemistry unit faces axe', *Financial Times*, 14 April 2003.

69. 'Oxford signals end of one-on-one tutorials', *The Times*, 26 October 2002. How far the
proposed cuts were forced by finance, and how far by an increasing reluctance on the part of
dons to teach sixteen hours a week is unclear. For an outraged view of the burden of the tutorial system for dons, see Lawrence Goldman, 'Stint Reform: A Rejoinder', *Oxford Magazine*,
noughth week, Hilary Term 2003, p.3.

70. 'Oxford considers top-up tuition fees to cut deficit', *Sunday Times*, 23 June 2002.

71. The suggestion allegedly made the civil servants nervous. One suspects they need not
worry. Congregation would almost certainly vote down such a move; the scientists would fear
for their beloved research contracts. This fear would be based on the assumption that government would threaten universities that privatised with the prospect of being ineligible for
research grants. If, of course, Oxford, Cambridge, Imperial and UCL all declared themselves
independent – a highly unlikely possibility – then there would be a most interesting stand-off.

deficit;[72] and the AUT issued a list of universities in danger of closing: Luton, South Bank, Lincoln, Greenwich, Hull, North London and Coventry. Bristol and Durham were facing serious funding crises.[73] As the cash-strapped old universities were forced to take more students, the numbers at less distinguished universities were threatened.[74]

Margaret Hodge moved to alter the rules about goals and targets for universities as it became abundantly clear that parents were moving house to enrol their children at the best state schools, or, like the Prime Minister, using 'opted out' schools, or taking their children out of private schools to do the sixth form at state schools. She weakened the emphasis on state schools and postcodes and put more emphasis on parental income and social class and whether parents had been to university (to be held against the children).[75] Further evidence of elitism in the eyes of the left was the discovery that top universities were not only highly selective academically and took (in their view) too many middle-class students from independent schools, but they had high graduation rates. The less elite universities did not; in other words they had much higher drop-out

72. 'Shock for campus as deficit hits £9.8m', *Times Higher Education Supplement*, 22 February 2002. Nationally, however, seventy-two per cent opposed top-up fees. '72 per cent oppose top-up fees, poll reveals', *Times Higher Education Supplement*, 10 January 2003.

73. 'Top universities face cash crisis', *Times Higher Education Supplement*, 27 June 2003.

74. In 2003 Leeds and Liverpool each took 2000 more students, Nottingham, 15 per cent more, Birmingham 11 per cent, Bristol and Manchester 9 per cent more. Meanwhile numbers at University of North London (now incorporated in London Metropolitan University) fell 29 per cent. Nationally numbers applying for higher national diplomas fell 23.4 per cent. Only 1250 people applied for foundation degrees. 'Ex-polys hit as elite mops up', *Times Higher Education Supplement*, 14 February 2003. Presumably the less well-known institutions were hit in two ways: financially poorer students were discouraged from attending universities by the introduction of fees and the abolition of maintenance grants; and those that did pay opted for the better-known institutions since fees were identical.

75. 'Universities told to look harder for poor students', *Financial Times*, 18 December 2002. On the postcode provisions, see 'Bending the rules', *Economist*, 24 August 2002.

ratios. Was it that they taught badly, or took unprepared students (in the summer of 2002 the Sunday papers reported that the Universities of Westminster and Portsmouth had both admitted students to read sociology who had failed all their A levels)[76] or that they accepted students who (or whose parents) had no real interest in the life of the mind?[77] Such concerns caused scepticism about the apparent obsession with the political goal of ever-increasing numbers in higher education.

The Labour goal of fifty per cent of all students in higher or even further education was increasingly questioned. As Baroness Warnock, a former Mistress of Girton College, Cambridge, put it:

76.　At the University of Lincoln, twenty-five per cent of those studying tourism failed the first year and another twenty per cent the second. Of those admitted, half did not have A levels but GNVQs; those with A levels had an average score of 12, the equivalent of three Ds. At Liverpool John Moores, thirty-seven per cent of those studying politics failed or dropped out. The average A levels were 14.5, the equivalent of a C and two Ds. 'Lower entry standards revealed at universities', *The Times*, 11 January 2002.

77.　At fourteen universities, at least a quarter of the students were failing to obtain any kind of qualification: Anglia, Central Lancashire, East London, Glasgow Caledonian, Glamorgan, Greenwich, Huddersfield, London Guildhall, Luton, North London, Paisley, South Bank, Sunderland and Thames Valley. The universities with the best graduation rates were almost exclusively those universities under attack for failing to take a high enough percentage of state school students: Bristol, Cambridge, Durham, Edinburgh, Exeter, Leeds, Nottingham, Oxford, Oxford Brookes, Reading, St Andrews, Southampton, University College London and West of England. 'One in four students fails to stay the course', *Daily Telegraph*, 18 December 2002. In London, the University of North London, which had 97 per cent state school students expected a 45 per cent drop-out rate; University College London, which had 60 per cent, had a 7 per cent drop-out rate. But the pattern was irregular. City University, with 81 per cent state school students, had a 5 per cent drop-out rate and the London School of Economics, with 66 per cent state students, a 4 per cent drop-out rate. 'Elite colleges admit too few poor students', *Evening Standard*, 18 December 2002. Statistically, using A at A level as 10, down to E as 2, in 1999/2000, Cambridge averaged 29.7, Oxford 29.5, LSE 28.2, Imperial 27.9, Bristol 26.5. For 1998/9, the bottom universities were Thames Valley 10.6, North London 11.1, Luton 11.2, London Guildhall 11.3, East London 11.7, South Bank 11.8, Brighton 12.0. Highest HEFCE postcode premiums as a percentage of teaching grant in 2002/3 were Sunderland 2.7, Wolverhampton 2.6, Derby 2.3, Salford 2.3, Teesside 2.3, Liverpool John Moores 2.3, Northumbria 2.2. 'Means testify to the trends', *Times Higher Education Supplement*, 7 June 2002.

I believe that, one way or another, we should stop filling our universities with students who displayed no interest in academic matters at school, whose talents are more practical than theoretical, and who will not change. They may proceed to university for a variety of motives: because they are very bright; because they like the idea of student life; or because they have been led to believe in what has been referred to as a 'myth' that obtaining a degree will make them necessarily individually more employable and lead to a better salary. But too few of them have any interest in continuing to learn. They have no very clear idea of the point of what they are going to learn or what they will do with it. For many of them, their years at university will, if they stick them out, be expensive and a waste of time.[78]

There was also increasing questioning of what university was for. While Oxford was still singled out for hostility for living in the age of Waugh's *Brideshead Revisited*, a cursory glance at the student guides to universities and colleges implied that the typical English university increasingly revolved around an alcoholic yobbish culture. Apparently, being inebriated without the assistance of a dinner jacket was politically acceptable. The 'uni' had become a rite of passage, at least for Middle England. Clearly what the Anderson Report had warned might become 'a kind of National Service' had in fact occurred without a clear vision of its purpose.

Even Oxford slowly woke up to the dangers. There was evidence that Oxford was losing students to US universities. (Previously it had

---

78. *Parl. Deb.*, House of Lords, vol. 641, cols 795–6 (27 November 2002). For a similar viewpoint, see Graham Zellick, Opinion, *Guardian Education*, 20 November 2001. It was all vaguely reminiscent of Robert Hutchins, Dean of the Yale Law School in the 1920s and President of the University of Chicago in the 1930s and 1940s, who is alleged to have said that the only hope for higher education in America was to give every child a BA at birth. See generally, Robert M. Hutchins, *The Higher Learning in America* (New Haven, CT, 1936).

been assumed that it was parents whose children could not get into a good English university who chose the American option.) It was argued that in a global economy, when American, Japanese and German corporations had taken over substantial parts of British industry, while the American, Swiss and Dutch had taken over substantial portions of the City, it would not be so threatening if British R & D migrated to the States and English students increasingly sought out their undergraduate education at American colleges and universities.[79] Harvard and Yale[80] both now provide need-blind admissions to UK students and provide a package of scholarship, loan and work. Stanford, among other universities, announced a programme of full scholarships for talented EU students.[81] The idea of America taking the cream was not an argument that was to appeal to Secretary Clarke.

In a powerful lecture at Magdalen College, Oxford ('How to Save the British Universities') Martin Wolf of the *Financial Times* made a strong case for top-up fees.[82] Sir Colin Lucas, the Vice-Chancellor of Oxford, in a courageous document,[83] added his support, although

79.   Robert Stevens, 'Urgent lessons in adequate funding', *Financial Times*, 19 November 2002. See 'Students look to US universities to beat fees rise', *The Times*, 7 February 2003; 'Sign up here for Princeton', *ibid*; and 'Go west young man', leader, *ibid*.

80.   Letter to alumni from President Richard C. Levin of Yale, 28 March 2003. For three and four good A levels the BA course might be shortened from four to three years.

81.   Michael Burleigh, 'Few of you would get an interview here', *Times Higher Education Supplement*, 4 April 2003.

82.   The Singer and Friedlander Lecture at Magdalen College, 26 September 2002. France, the UK and Germany ranked almost at the bottom of the table in terms of percentage of GDP spent on higher education (1.13 per cent, 1.11 per cent, 1.05 per cent respectively). The average for the OECD countries was 1.60 per cent; the US 2.29 per cent. In terms of public spending on tertiary education as a percentage of GDP, the UK (0.83 per cent) came below France (1.01 per cent) and Germany (0.97 per cent). Canada spent 1.53 per cent; the OECD average was 0.93 per cent. In per-student expenditure, the US spent $19,802 per student, Switzerland $16,563, Australia $11,539, the UK $9,699, Germany $9,481, France $7,226. The OECD average was $11,720. See also 'The ruin of Britain's universities', *Economist*, 16 November 2002.

83.   'University Funding and Fees: From the Vice-Chancellor', *Oxford University Gazette*, 21 November 2002.

whether he would have been supported by Congregation was unclear; the tradition of the dons' parliament was generally to back the wrong horse.[84] Certainly Charles Clarke had little to fear from the Conservatives. Iain Duncan Smith seemed to be opposed to top-up fees; Kenneth Clarke, who had abolished the binary divide without a clear vision for the future, was circling again, looking to take over the leadership from IDS. He now wanted to abolish all fees, while other members of his party talked of slashing public spending by twenty per cent. It would presumably be a grim time indeed for universities if the Tories ever gained power again,[85] although with probably only two years to go before the next election the party still had, at that time, no policy on universities. That may have been irrelevant as the polls suggested another victory for New Labour.

Meanwhile, the Department for Education and Skills – as it was by then called – delayed decisions on funding for future years, and there was talk of universities declaring their independence, which as corporate charities, they legally could do. Surrey allegedly talked of going entirely independent; as did Birmingham, if it would still qualify for research funds.[86] When Margaret Hodge told universities that their demand for £9.9 billion was 'cloud cuckoo land' there was irritation,[87] but when the Chancellor of the Exchequer

---

84. There was a postal vote on this very issue. Ultimately, Oxford dons, unlike Cambridge dons, supported top-up fees.

85. The most intelligent analysis from a Conservative was from Robert Jackson MP, a former Higher Education Minister. He argued that Conservatives should support top-up fees because (1) 'Conservative philosophy is to keep the size of institutions as small as necessary, and the burden of tax as low as possible'; (2) Conservatives want public services that are accountable to users and (3) Conservatives favour 'Burke's little platoons'. The universities have 'only very recently been nationalised – with the usual deplorable consequences. It would be perverse for Conservatives to oppose measures of de-nationalisation from a Labour government'. Letter, *Daily Telegraph*, 23 November 2002.

86. 'Universities threaten to go private', *The Times*, 30 October 2002.

87. 'Dream on, Hodge replies to VC's demand for cash', *Times Higher Education Supplement*, 20 September 2002.

offered six per cent increases for each of three years, the chances of any university going it alone became minimal. England had a commendable concern for its Welfare State, as befits a humane society, and, for all the talk of the enterprise culture, England remains a risk-averse society.

As the debate on the White Paper heated up, however, there were other matters to be dealt with. The fiasco in 2002 over A grades led the government to push for a British Baccalaureate,[88] which would apparently merge GCSE, A levels and vocational courses. While such a change would threaten the traditional universities, with their single-subject in-depth degrees, it would be welcomed by the state sector of secondary education. Since GCSE was effectively failed[89] by fifty per cent of students (more than sixty per cent in the state schools), the government needed an exam which could include more vocational subjects. As Secretary Clarke put it in introducing the new White Paper on Secondary Education: 'We can no longer tolerate an artificial divide between the world of education and the world of work.' The new syllabus would de-emphasise exams and emphasise continuous evaluation and objective tests. Those were blurrings which would help the less well-taught students at the

---

88. 'A levels and GCSEs to be replaced by British bac', *Daily Telegraph*, 22 January 2003; 'A levels to be "recast" in drive to cut school drop-outs', *Financial Times*, 22 January 2003; 'Baccalaureate will replace A levels and GCSEs by 2010', *The Times*, 22 January 2003; 'Colleges gain a role in 14–19 reforms', *The Times Higher Education Supplement*, 24 January 2003. The A level may survive in an alternative form, but the old academic universities could be further weakened. Rather than the 'Bac', the Labour-leaning research institute, Demos, suggested a 'learning licence' assessing the pupils' ability to learn. 'Call for "learning" licence to replace A levels', *Financial Times*, 7 March 2003. The Tomlinson Committee is now at work on the alternatives. The problem is the traditional one. Universities are anxious to have exams that distinguish the brightest students, and there is talk of the leading universities reestablishing entrance exams; many of the left-leaning educational and political establishment are interested in an egalitarian system that produces prizes for all. See Melanie Phillips, *All Must Have Prizes*, (London, 1996) p. 186.

89. That is to say, failed to get six core GCSEs at A–C grade.

typical state school. All students would have to study citizenship and IT; history, geography, and modern languages for those over fourteen were to become optional. Students would be able to spend two days a week on the shop floor or in some other work situation. The traditional English secondary model – 'the bog-standard comprehensive', Alastair Campbell called them – is scheduled by 2010 to have been replaced by a mixture of technical schools and specialist schools.

A revolution in secondary education along these lines may be needed. If it were to occur, however, it would also require a serious analysis of what the English think universities are for. This could be achieved in one of two ways: if the universities remain under central government control and funding, a far-reaching Master Plan would be needed, together with a massive increase in funding. Or the universities might be given more freedom through being exposed to the market, with funding from a variety of sources, and then be allowed to work out their individual roles.[90]

---

90. More complex still for politicians is what is to happen to the fifty percent of the population who do not go on to further education at eighteen or the thirty percent who do not stay in any form of education after sixteen.

10. *The Final Act:*
Build-up, Report, Reaction

The time between the appointment of Charles Clarke in October 2002 and the publication of the White Paper in January 2003 was a feisty one. As we have already seen, the period was dominated by the increasing friction between the Chancellor and the Prime Minister. The *Sunday Telegraph* – not always to be trusted in reporting political battles in the Labour Party – even went so far as to suggest that Gordon Brown was using the issues of foundation hospitals and top-up fees as a way of toppling Tony Blair and seizing control of the Labour Party.[1] While Brown was moving to the left to collect the anti-intellectual votes of the class-obsessed Labour backbenchers (in 1997 he had talked supportively of the research universities), Clarke found he had to throw bones to the same group in an effort to buy off the attacks. Thus Clarke

---

1.   Matthew d'Ancona, 'A "coup" by Gordon? Tony's people believe it is coming', *Daily Telegraph*, 19 January 2003; Andrew Rawnsley, 'Tony Blair's midlife crisis', *Observer*, 29 December 2002; 'Will top-up fees be the issue that finally divides Blair and Brown?', *Daily Telegraph*, 21 January 2003. Probably the most dramatic attack on Blair came in the *New Statesman*, owned by Brownite Geoffrey Robinson: John Kampfner, 'What is the point of Tony Blair?', *New Statesman*, 21 July 2003; Peter Dunn, 'So were the Tories right after all?', *ibid.* (suggesting that Blair had psychological problems); 'The Blair question', leader, *ibid.*

appeared to be willing to abolish the last remaining grammar schools.[2] Ironically this came at a moment when a Department for Education study showed that the grammar schools far outperformed the comprehensives in providing value-added education from eleven to fourteen. Apparently selectivity added to academic achievement.[3] Excellence had reared its ugly head; it must be elitist. The new study led Frank Dobson to demand that in the next Labour manifesto there should be a proviso that the last grammar schools should be abolished![4]

Not only was there Gordon Brown's ambition to be taken into account; there was his obsession with micro-managing all aspects of the domestic economy. The autumn of 2002 was indeed a stormy period. Charles Clarke's November discussion paper clearly had the desired effect. It may well be that Tony Blair and Andrew Adonis favoured a naked up front fee, but Charles Clarke thought it would never fly politically. By December 2002, the *Guardian* reported that, in the light of the Brown opposition, together with back-bench and student protests, the Prime Minister had given up on up front fees.[5] The alternative, pushed by one of Blair's gurus, LSE Director Anthony Giddens, was variable fees to be paid through government loans then repaid though the tax system, the so-called Crawford-Barr scheme.[6] This then became the position of

2. 'Clarke refuses to guarantee safety of grammars', *Daily Mail*, 20 January 2003. Tony Blair later tried to reassure voters about the safety of the grammars. *Financial Times*, 30 January 2003.

3. 'Grammar Schools top for "added value"', *Daily Telegraph*, 23 January 2003.

4. A report from a group of charities, not surprisingly, discovered that where there were grammar schools, the remaining state schools had worse GCSE results. 'Charities call for ban on grammars', *Daily Telegraph*, 25 March 2003.

5. 'Blair signals retreat on student top-up fees', *Guardian*, 5 December 2002.

6. Anthony Giddens, 'There is a third way', *ibid*.

the Prime Minister and his Secretary for Education. It was anathema to backbench Labour MPs, because it would suggest that not all universities were identical, as well as to Gordon Brown, who sensed that he might lose fiscal and administrative control of the universities.[7] Nor was the idea attractive that unsuccessful universities might be allowed to go out of business – a suggestion of Higher Education Minister, Margaret Hodge.[8] When Secretary Clarke asked why only twenty per cent of US higher education institutions were allowed to give graduate degrees, compared with eighty per cent in the UK, there was gnashing of teeth by those in institutions who thought they might be relegated to teaching only.[9] In fact since CNAA days in the early seventies they had been allowed to give such advanced degrees, so the suggestion was at best a paper tiger.

It was, however, around 10 January 2003 that the fireworks really started. On that day, the *Guardian* reported that Clarke was going to propose top-up fees of up to £3,000, paid through loans which were repayable later, coupled with the restoration of maintenance grants for the poor.[10] The previous day, Clarke had been given a hard time by Labour MPs opposed to the scheme and over the weekend warfare began to break out in the Cabinet. The Chancellor still wanted a graduate tax and was thought to be egging on the backbenchers to oppose the new top-up scheme, now rebranded differential fees. His people leaked that there was instead to be a graduate

7.   'Up-front university tuition fees may be replaced by charge on graduates', *Financial Times*, 8 January 2003.

8.   'Unpopular universities "should go to the wall"', *The Times*, 10 September 2002.

9.   'Charles Clarke vs. the universities', *The Independent: Higher Education*, 9 January 2003. See also 'Pretty Poly?', *Economist*, 22 March 2002: 'Polytechnics turned into universities. Now they may be turning back again.'

10.   'Top-up fees row settled with plan for graduate tax', *Guardian*, 10 January 2003.

tax.[11] By Wednesday, the Chancellor's spin doctors were leaking the view that the need for additional funding had been overblown, there was no need to make the decision until the next Parliament[12] (when presumably Brown would be Prime Minister) and there was little point in giving more money to universities until they were better run and took more poor students. On Thursday, the Cabinet Sub-Committee, chaired by John Prescott, met and there was a stand-off between Clarke and Brown, who was not accustomed to 'spending' ministers standing up to him. The spin doctors went to work.[13] The following day, after Brown had, perhaps somewhat reluctantly, supported Blair on the war in Iraq, the Treasury leaked the news that Brown had vetoed the White Paper on higher education.[14] Some thought that was the *quid pro quo* for the support on Iraq, but No. 10 replied angrily that the differential fee was accepted and the White Paper would appear.[15] In addition to the return of maintenance grants,

11.   'Showdown looms over university top-up fees', *Financial Times*, 11-12 January 2003; Philip Stephens, 'Frost in the Downing Street trenches', *Financial Times*, 13 January 2003.

12.   'We want to keep this open as a possibility until the next Parliament when the key financing decisions will be taken.' 'Brown funding fear may delay university reform', *The Times*, 15 January 2003.

13.   The main BBC News had its political commentator say that differential fees would be politically unacceptable because it would allow a two-tier system of universities, allowing Oxford to charge more 'because it is socially exclusive and thinks it's better'. BBC, 6 o'clock News, 16 January 2003.

14.   'Brown veto on plan for top-up fees', *Guardian*, 17 January 2003; 'Ministers deadlocked over university fees', *Financial Times*, 17 January 2003. A Treasury spokesman said: 'The whole question of differential fees vs. graduate tax is still outstanding.' No. 10 said it was settled. That evening, BBC's Newsnight trotted out various Labour MPs to say that a two-tier system would never be acceptable and that Vice-Chancellors must not be allowed freedom over fees.

15.   'Blair in slap-down for Brown over top-up fees', *Daily Telegraph*, 18 January 2003. 'Universities must take poor to charge extra: £3,000 top-up fee to go ahead as Blair sides against Brown', *id.*; 'No. 10 confident of solving top-up fees equation', *Financial Times*, 18/19 January 2003. This last reported that it was more the other ministers rather than Brown who had been upset by the solution. 'Ministers display unity as Clarke emerges strengthened', *ibid.*, 23 January 2003.

backbench MPs were to be placated by a regulator,[16] who would ensure that universities took the requisite number of poor students, or they would lose their right to charge differential fees.[17]

The Times[18] produced a thoughtful analysis of the future of universities, arguing first, that while social mix was important, 'any attempt to regulate the social composition of students would compromise both the principle of admission on merit and the independence of the institutions'; second, that 'a sizeable segment of the costs involved in acquiring a degree should be absorbed by the students and not by their parents or the taxpayer'; third, that there was a need for 'maintenance grants to be awarded to those from deprived backgrounds'; fourth, that 'differential, or top up fees are logical', but would require regulation; and fifth, that a long-term solution was essential.[19] Over the weekend, the right-wing press continued to examine the Chancellor's behaviour. The Chancellor's leaking, which was denied, was described by one Cabinet Minister: 'This is destabilisation leading, with the help of Gordon's newspaper allies, to a coup. That is what it is all about: either upsetting Tony to the point where he jacks it in, or destabilisation where things go badly wrong

---

16. Wittily dubbed OFFTOFF by Damian Green, the Shadow Education Secretary. (The regulatory bodies for the privatised industries are known as OFTEL, OFWAT etc.)

17. Ironically, this was the very day that George Bush attacked universities in the US for insisting on having preferential quotas for minority students. 'Bush assails university's "quotas" policy on minorities', *International Herald Tribune*, 17 January 2003. Ironically too, it was the day that a Liberal Democrat plan was leaked, saying that top-up fees were unnecessary. Students would not be admitted directly to universities, but would have to attend a local two-year college and then compete for a university place. 'Lib Dem plan top-up-free degrees', *Guardian*, 17 January 2003.

18. 'Universities we deserve', leader, *The Times*, 18 January 2003.

19. The *Daily Telegraph* opined that the White Paper the following week 'should be judged by three criteria: excellence, access and independence. Mr. Clarke and Downing Street seem to have grasped the importance of at least the first two of these goals. There is, however, a danger that a typical New Labour compromise will emerge, one that generates too little cash to make a real difference to universities, but one that comes with so many strings that in practice their relationship with the state is even more terrible', 18 January 2003.

and people say it's time for a change.'[20] On the Sunday, Clarke admitted on television that students could end up with debts of £21,000 at the maximum, with the average being £12,000 to £14,000.

Martin Wolf, who had advocated the urgency of saving all universities, welcomed the proposals. He warned, however, there were two enemies: first, the Labour backbenchers; second, and far more serious, the English middle classes, who wanted something for nothing.[21] He clearly was right. In the student demonstrations before Christmas, the *Daily Telegraph* published a picture of an upper-class young woman carrying a placard 'Save My Daddy's Money'.[22] The *Daily Mail*, the downscale right-wing paper, reported the proposals on page one under the banner: '£21,000: The staggering debt facing graduates under Labour's plan for top-up fees.'[23] The *Guardian* reported the political response of the left. One Labour MP said: 'This goes to the very heart of the party. This is all driven by Downing Street and it's about class and background. It's going to get intensely personal.' As the *Economist* noted: 'the universities, especially those with any claim to elite status, turn the Chancellor into a raving Jacobin.'[24] The Liberal Democrats announced that top-up fees were a 'huge disincentive'.[25] The lead-

20.   'Cabinet Ministers accuse Chancellor of "coup" plot', *Sunday Telegraph*, 19 January 2003

21.   'The omens look good for UK universities', *Financial Times*, 20 January 2003. For the backlash by Middle England, see Martin Bentham, 'The real university challenge', *Sunday Telegraph*, 24 November 2002; 'Top-up fees will finish parents', *Evening Standard*, 19 November 2002.

22.   5 December 2002

23.   20 January 2003.

24.   Bagehot, 'Equality or efficiency', *Economist*, 25 January 2003.

25.   Ian Gibson, Labour MP for Norwich, warned that it would be privatisation next. Ann Campbell, MP for Cambridge, added: 'If you end up with a system where poor kids go to the expoly and the rich kids to Cambridge, it will be a disaster.' The centre of the party was more generous. Barry Sheerman, Labour Chair of the Commons Education Committee, pleaded: 'I hope Mr. Blair will come in, bang a few heads and say "come on, this is one of the most significant strategy documents of two Labour governments".' *Daily Telegraph*, 18 January 2003.

ing universities were upset by the regulator to monitor admissions of the poor.[26] Sir Richard Sykes, former businessman and Rector of Imperial College, announced: 'This is social engineering at its worst. It will bring chaos into the system. They are insisting we take socially deprived kids who have not been educated properly.'[27] Meanwhile, the idea of differential fees was vigorously attacked by the National Association of Teachers in Further and Higher Education ('Clarke and Hodge want to create narrow functional and utilitarian institutions for the poor while sending the rich students to a British Ivy League'[28]), while it was condemned by the Vice-Chancellor of the University of Coventry as 'social and economic elitism in the extreme'.[29] The Vice-Chancellors of the new universities could not agree, however, on whether the proposal would set back higher education thirty or forty years.[30]

The press was similarly divided. The *Daily Telegraph* fumed in a leader about 'the state commissar ("access regulator") to vet their

---

26. 'Plan for university regulator branded a disgrace', *The Times*, 20 January 2003. They were supported by the *Financial Times*: 'Degrees of access: universities cannot make up for poorly performing schools', 23 January 2003. Roughly forty-three per cent of middle-class students have two A levels; only nineteen per cent of those from poorer backgrounds. See also 'Oxbridge alarm at quotas', *The Times*, 23 January 2003; 'Private school fear bias under top-up fee rules', *The Times*, 27 January 2003.

27. 'Graduates could be left in debt for 30 years', *Daily Telegraph*, 20 January 2003.

28. 'Integrity is not safe in hands of "crass" government', *Times Higher Education Supplement*, 30 May 2003.

29. 'Universities must take poor to charge extra', *The Times*, 18 January 2003.

30. Earlier, Malcolm McVicar, the Vice-Chancellor of Central Lancashire, had opined: 'Differential fees would be a disaster for British higher education. They would destroy equality of access and mitigate widening participation . . . They would set higher education back 40 years.' 'V-Cs resigned to top-ups', *Times Higher Education Supplement*, 8 November 2002. See McVicar's later lament, 'Why has Mr. Clarke thrown us to market forces?', *Times Higher Education Supplement*, 14 February 2003. Professor Neil Buxton of the University of Hertfordshire said: 'The reforms are about ability to pay, not ability and will set back education in the country by thirty years.' *Financial Times*, 23 January 2003.

admissions procedures ... an approach ... generally confined to the Soviet bloc'.[31] Meanwhile, the editorial in the *Financial Times* glowed in support: 'High marks for university plans: clear thinking at last on higher education.'[32] Ultimately, the *Daily Telegraph*, known to the satirical magazine *Private Eye* as the 'Torygraph', reluctantly accepted that, with the exception of the regulator, the Clarke proposals were fair.[33] The *Daily Mail*, aimed at downscale Tory voters, was opposed,[34] while the so-called red-tops, the *Sun* and the *Mirror*, were upset at the threat of debt. The intellectual press, including this time the *Observer*, normally in the visceral left corner, came out in favour of the Clarke plan,[35] a support shared with *The Times*[36] and the *Economist*[37].

What then did the Clarke White Paper include?[38] The claim was that the new agenda would attract the talented from all backgrounds; give universities the freedom to compete on the world

---

31. 'No wonder dons – generally a left-leaning constituency – are so opposed to the idea.. [the] difficulty is that the maintained sector is falling further and further behind – not because of underfunding (total spending per pupil at about £5,000 a year, is now comparable to many independent day schools), but because of government meddling, poor teaching and lack of ambition.' Editorial, 'Clarke fails the funding test', *Daily Telegraph*, 21 January 2003. The correct average figures at the secondary level are £4,855 in the state sector; and £6,364 in the private sector. Anthony Smith, 'Will they never learn?', *Evening Standard*, 21 January 2003. No one seemed interested in the fact that it is arguable that universities get less per student for teaching than secondary schools.

32. 21 January 2003.

33. 'Fees for freedom', *Daily Telegraph*, 23 January 2003.

34. 'Student debt as high as £50,000', *Daily Mail*, 23 January 2003.

35. 'Top-up fees are the right answer', *Observer*, 26 January 2003.

36. 'The right course', *The Times*, 23 January 2003.

37. 'The best men won: The government is doing the right thing by universities', *Economist*, 25 January 2003.

38. Department for Education and Skills, *The Future of Higher Education*, Cm. 5735 (January 2003).

stage; and make the system of supporting students fairer. It was accepted that there were many fine things about English universities, but that they were in serious difficulties. As might be expected, the Report emphasised research and its links to business. While research was strong 'it is declining', which the Report attributed to the failure to concentrate it in a limited number of institutions. Moreover, good researchers needed good facilities (and these were dated, inadequate for modern research and lacking in maintenance) and adequate salaries to hold the best researchers (more than a quarter of Fellows of the Royal Society – in a country which now rarely has Nobel Prize winners, the highest accolade normally achieved by scientists – worked abroad).

The White Paper also acknowledged that teaching had also declined as staff-student ratios had fallen from 1:10 in 1983 to 1:18 in 2000. Students wrote fewer essays and had less direct contact with staff. There was at last a recognition that skills training and shortages in industry might well be best met at the higher technical level, rather than at the degree level, but the status of a degree over a professional qualification had drawn students into degrees and caused the shortage of technicians. 'We must break this cycle of low esteem.' It was reported that nine out of ten students with two A levels went on to university. At the same time UCAS reported that media studies, cinema studies and sports science were all booming, while the numbers wanting to study biology, chemistry, maths, physics and engineering continued to drop.[39] At the same time, the fact that 'young people from professional backgrounds are over five times more likely to enter higher education than those

---

39.   'Lower entry standards revealed at universities', *Daily Telegraph*, 11 January 2002. For the decline in maths and science teaching, see 'Hard numbers', *Economist*, 19 April 2003. The 2003 A level results confirmed this trend.

from unskilled backgrounds' had to be addressed. The paper was vague on how to encourage disadvantaged groups into universities without drying up the supply of technicians, but extending maintenance grants to further education colleges was obviously a step in the right direction.

The Report confirmed a six per cent increase in real terms in funding for each of the following three years. There was then a remarkable confession: 'The Government accepts that it has been partly responsible for the failure to have an honest recognition of universities' different roles.' At last there was to be a vision for higher education.[40] With that chapter on the need for reform, the Report launched into its demand for research, which in future was to be even more clearly based in the leading institutions, although they would be encouraged to form consortia with others. The amount for research was to be dramatically increased, the RAE (Research Assessment Exercise) greatly strengthened – there was to be a new 6* rating for excellence[41] – and the Government was clearly relying on a new Report from Sir Gareth Roberts to justify the changes it was planning.[42] His Report, when it appeared, called for a tripartite approach to funding of research in universities. Where less than two per cent of the universities' budget came from research, the university would be excluded from the RAE. This would mean that universities such as London Metropolitan, Leeds Metropolitan, Thames Valley, Central England, Derby, Lincoln, Staffordshire, Teesside and Wolverhampton would cease to receive

40. *The Future of Higher Education*, pp. 21–2.

41. An idea initially abandoned after the Scots, who had apparently not been consulted about the Clarke White Paper, protested. It was eventually reinstated by extrapolating from earlier RAEs.

42. Formerly Vice-Chancellor of the University of Sheffield and now President of Wolfson College, Oxford and a member of HEFCE.

any research funds from HEFCE. Universities with a mid range of research would be assessed by discussions with expert panels (the Green Channel). The Research Assessment Exercise would apply only to major research universities and would, after the initial decision, be based on a relatively light touch.[43] The excluded universities were outraged,[44] and even institutions like Bristol were worried that research, in future, would be limited to the golden triangle – Oxford, Cambridge and London.[45]

There was in the White Paper, as one would expect, a chapter on links with business,[46] both in terms of research and transferring technology. This meant an increase in the Higher Education Innovation Fund and links with Regional Development Agencies. Equally important, however, was to be an emphasis on the development of technical skills. The newer universities were congratulated on what they had already achieved (fifty-five per cent of all first-degree and diploma students at the University of Brighton undertook formal work experience) and there was to be a heavy emphasis on two-year foundation degrees. (Such degrees were dismissed by NATFHE as 'a ruse to ... give working class students an inferior qualification wrongly branded a "degree".'[47]) Links with business

---

43.　'RAE reform to shut out one in three', *Times Higher Education Supplement*, 30 May 2003; 'Sorting swans from ducklings' *Guardian Higher*, 3 June 2003.

44.　Peter Scott, Vice-Chancellor of Kingston University declared: 'The RAE is about more than grants, it's about reputation and staff morale.' *Times Higher Education Supplement*, 30 May 2003.

45.　See, for instance, 'Gold rush', *Guardian, Higher*, 3 June 2003. Oxford, Cambridge, Imperial, UCL and Kings College absorb over half the research funds. During the summer of 2003 the proposed concentration was diluted, allowing institutions such as Bristol and Southampton into the charmed circle.

46.　*The Future of Higher Education*, ch. 3.

47.　'New degree is a "cheap and inferior con"', *Times Higher Education Supplement*, 3 May 2003.

were to be explored by Richard Lambert, formerly editor of the *Financial Times*, appointed by Chancellor Brown in 2002, allegedly without consulting the Secretary of Education. Secretary Clarke was, however, supportive of broadening the enquiry to investigate the management of universities – an increasing obsession of the Chancellor's.[48]

While the tone of the White Paper pointed to increasing independence for universities, the hand of the *dirigiste* Department for Education and Skills was also evident. In terms of teaching,[49] the government's commitment to run quality controls was reaffirmed. The NUS was co-opted to develop a survey of student evaluation. To placate those universities whose interest in research would be dampened down, there were to be extra funds for rewarding good teaching. The system of accrediting all university teachers by 2006 remained, there was to be a national system of external examiners by 2004/5. There was talk of a teaching quality academy – a national body to reward good teaching by 2004, together with well-funded centres of excellence in teaching; by 2004/5, the title of university would be awarded to universities that did not award research degrees.[50] (The justification for this was the analogy with the

---

48. He was reportedly still obsessed with the governance of Oxbridge, still harbouring doubts about the Laura Spence affair and the much publicized activities of the Chaplain of Pembroke. The Chancellor was also concerned that if the variable fee cap went over £3000, Oxbridge could exploit its monopoly position. At the same time there was support for his concerns about management. Sir Geoffrey Holland, the former Vice-Chancellor of Exeter, said that in no other sector were senior managers 'so amateur, so apparently unconcerned' about leadership skills. The Chancellor was also alleged to be fuming about Cambridge's handling of the MIT grant.

49. *The Future of Higher Education*, ch. 4.

50. And in the spring of 2003 the names of six new potential non-research universities were announced: University College Worcester, University College Northampton, Canterbury Christ Church University College, Buckingham Chilterns University College, Liverpool Hope and the London Institution. They are expected to come 'on stream' by 2004. The announcement by Margaret Hodge also envisaged the right of companies to gain degree-granting powers and 'for profit universities'. 'Dozens of colleges invited to become universities', *The Times*, 4 June 2003.

California State University System.)[51] For good measure, there was talk of abolishing classes of degrees; and of a national system for student complaints. The QAA survived but basically for problem areas. For the typical university the Agency was there to ensure that quality was assessed rather than to assess quality itself. There was to be more money for staff pay – providing institutions had a merit system. It looked as if, after nearly a century of a national pay scale, each university might establish its own pay scale. When, however, Imperial College took the first tentative steps in this direction, there was panic in the ranks, particularly at the AUT.

In terms of numbers, the goal had become 'towards fifty per cent'.[52] Much of the expansion, however, was to come through 'two-year work-focused foundation degrees'. Many of these were to be in further education colleges. 'We are not choosing between more plumbers and more graduates. We need both, and we need to help individuals to make sensitive and appropriate choices.'[53] The goal was to make ninety per cent of young people ready for higher education or skilled employment; but the real growth was to be at the associate professional or higher education level. Thus, with more top-skimming of funds by the Department, there were to be premium payments for those institutions offering associate degrees; and employers were to be encouraged to hire from two-year programmes rather than three-year ones.[54] An American credit system would be used to support such developments.

51. *The Future of Higher Education*, p. 55. For the list of further education colleges, which teach higher education courses and wish to be the new polys, see 'Colleges bid to become the new polys', *Times Higher Education Supplement*, 20 September 2002.

52. Ch. 5.

53. *Ibid*, p. 58.

54. For an attack on this top-skimming, see 'The University's response to the Government's White Paper, *The Future of Higher Education*,' *Oxford University Gazette*, supplement 1, 28 May 2003.

Access loomed large.[55] This meant admission procedures that were 'professional, fair and transparent',[56] and HEFCE was instructed to support the additional costs for non-traditional students. 'We will appoint a Higher Education Access Regulator, who will develop a framework for Access Arrangements for each institution. Only institutions making satisfactory progress on access will be able to participate in the Graduate Contribution Scheme from 2006.'[57] Emphasis was to be placed on urging students to stay on after sixteen and 'Second Chance' programmes for older candidates. To placate the Chancellor and the bureaucrats in the Department, Oxford and Cambridge were encouraged to centralise admissions,[58] putting yet another nail in the coffin of the dying collegiate university. In terms of access data, the government wanted to move the goalposts from 'social class, postcode and state/private school' to 'parents' income, parents' level of

55.   *The Future of Higher Education*, ch. 6.

56.   Secretary Clarke appears to have taken on board the suggestions of David VandeLinde, the American Vice-Chancellor of Warwick University, that an American-style admission system is preferable. This would take into account not only A levels, but references, sport, music, outside activities, etc. 'University places may be decided on pupils' broad CVs', *Financial Times*, 24 January 2003. Presumably, the one missing thing by US standards will be details of parents' or siblings' connections (and gifts) to the university! Ironically many at Oxbridge would claim that this broader approach to admissions parallels the much reviled Oxbridge system of admissions.

57.   P .68.

58.   Secretary Clarke said: 'Oxford and Cambridge should be looking to create a modern image of themselves to get applications from the best and brightest, irrespective of their social class ... The *Brideshead Revisited* image which Oxford sometimes transmits is not appropriate for that modern image ... Most people at Oxford and Cambridge believe it is outdated, but whether that is fully being conveyed to students and potential applicants is a matter for debate.' Damian Green, the Shadow Education Secretary accused Clarke of stoking 'class-war rhetoric'. 'Charles Clarke's sneering remarks about Oxford and Cambridge having to shed the Brideshead image shows a government completely out of touch with the reality of life in our universities.' 'Oxbridge must lose Brideshead reputation, says Clarke', *Evening Standard*, 8 April 2003; 'Universities must show they are open to all', *The Times*, 9 April 2003.

education and the average results of the school or college they attended.'[59]

As part of the deal, the up-front standard fee of £1,100 was abolished as of 2006, and universities were given the freedom to set fees up to £3,000, to be collected through the tax system, when earnings reached £15,000. How the increasing number of EU students, who are required to be treated as UK students, were to be dealt with, remained vague. For poorer students, the government would pay the first £1,100 of fees and pay £1,000 per annum in maintenance (on this the Secretary later offered further concessions). The Report also put great emphasis on universities building up endowments – the best way to ensure their independence in the long run.[60] There was even talk of matching funds from government. On fees, there was to be more help for part-time students, while students who entered the public services – NHS or teaching – might have their fees cancelled.

For the long-term however, the biggest U-turn in the relationship between government and universities came in chapter 7, 'Freedom and Funding':

59.   On this, see the irritation of an Old Etonian, with his children at a rural comprehensive that gets a number of Oxbridge places. David Thomas, 'Labour is waging a war against the children of the middle class', *Daily Telegraph*, 26 January 2003.

60.   The new Vice-Chancellor of Cambridge, Alison Richard, formerly Provost of Yale, implied that gifts from alumni could make top-up fees unnecessary. 'Steely veteran with a cold eye on bottom line', *Times Higher Education Supplement*, 6 December 2002. Shortly after her appointment, the dons, voting in Regent House, rejected a plan to give the new Vice-Chancellor more executive powers.

      By the early summer of 2003, Oxford announced its new Vice-Chancellor, John Hood, Vice-Chancellor of the University of Auckland; a former Rhodes scholar, engineer and businessman. 'Tough tests loom for Hood', *Times Higher Education Supplement*, 20 June 2003. His appointment coincided with increasing talk of Oxford taking fewer undergraduates and more post-graduates. 'Big shake-up and new V-C could take Oxford from ivy-clad to Ivy League', *ibid*.

      The Hood appointment was, in its own way, remarkable. Oxford has been the most in-bred of English universities. When the draft North Report was circulated to colleges for comment,

> *The Government is making an unprecedented investment in the*
> *universities and will stand by them in future spending reviews. But*
> *to be really successful, universities must be free to take responsibil-*
> *ity for their own strategic and financial future. Strong leadership*
> *and management, freed from excessive red tape, will help them not*
> *just to respond to change, but to drive it. And more financial free-*
> *dom will allow them to fund their plans, and unleash their power*
> *to drive world-class research, innovative knowledge transfer, excel-*
> *lent teaching ... and fair access.*

If this intent were carried through, it is arguable that the thrust of government policy towards universities for the last fifty years would have been noticeably reversed.

Certainly such a change was not immediately obvious in the aftermath of the Report. Indeed in the weeks after the Report there were developments which underlined the Gilbert-and-Sullivan quality of some parts of English public life. February saw concerns from the Centre for the Economics of Education within the Department for Education and Skills that the £3,000 top-up fees would 'widen the class divide'.[61] UCAS (the University and Colleges Admissions Service) announced it would require applicants to all universities to disclose parental earnings and education, which could then be held against those who had the temerity to have affluent or well-educated (or at least degreed) parents.[62] Edinburgh's Court then announced that state school students, if they were first-generation university applicants or came from a

---

the suggestion that an outsider might become Vice-Chancellor was described by one college as 'unthinkable' and by another as 'unconscionable'.

61.   Its Director, Steve Machin, was regarded as Chancellor Brown's 'Trojan horse' within the Department. 'Top-up fees will widen class divide', *Observer*, 23 February 2003.

62.   'Universities to ask: how disadvantaged are you?' *Daily Telegraph*, 17 February 2003.

poor school, would be given priority over private-school students.[63] Some dons at Oxford talked of not charging top-up fees in order to avoid being supervised by the Access Regulator.[64] The right-wing press was already singling out Bristol for discriminating against public-school students even if they were from minority groups.[65] To cool the excitement, a rumour was started that the Regulator would operate under the auspices of HEFCE.[66] The Prime Minister, in the midst of the Labour revolt over Iraq, said in the Commons – in apparent contradiction of Secretary Clarke – that admissions to universities should be based on merit, not class.[67]

March followed the same pattern. Sir Howard Newby, the Chief Executive of HEFCE and an important player in the Clarke Report, took various initiatives. (It was clear by this time that the role of HEFCE was to be the government's planning agency in higher education. Any residual role, inherited from the University Grants Committee, of being a buffer between universities and the state was largely dead.)[68] Contrary to the platitudinous concerns of

---

63. 'Edinburgh to put state pupils first', *The Times*, 19 February 2003.

64. Ian Rumfitt, 'A Mess of Pottage', *Oxford Magazine*, fourth week, Hilary Term 2003, p.1.

65. See the case of Rudi Singh. 'University snubs star private school pupil', *Sunday Times*, 23 February 2003. And see editorial, 'Universities choose failure', *ibid*: 'This case is every bit as significant as that of Laura Spence.'

66. 'Ministers moves to calm Vice-Chancellors' fears over new university regulator', *Financial Times*, 5 February 2003, implying that the regulator would operate under HEFCE.

67. 'Choose on merit, universities told', *Daily Telegraph*, 27 February 2003. And see editorial 'Answer to the academic question', *ibid*.

68. Following the Clarke White Paper, HEFCE produced a draft strategic plan. HEFCE's planning document saw four purposes of higher education: improving competitiveness; generating wealth; improving the quality of life; and 'improving social cohesion, through greater inclusiveness and shared values'. HEFCE, *HEFCE Strategic Plan 2003–08*, April 2003. As the vigorous Oxford University response noted: 'The draft strategic plan for 2003–8 marks a further step away from being a body principally concerned with providing one stream of public funding to higher education, towards being a body responsible to the planning of higher education, including its overall size and shape, and future strategic development. This reflects the

Universities UK, Newby said bluntly that 'we cannot sustain world-class research in ninety universities'. He also continued arguing for a £5,000 cap for top-up fees; £3,000 would not allow real differentiation. There was indeed increasing evidence that most universities, old and new, would be forced by financial circumstances to charge £3,000. The Office of Fair Trading was already muttering about violations of the Competition Act's provisions against price fixing.[69] Sir Howard was also talking of requiring universities to take a specific number of working-class students.

This last proposal had the middle classes and dons agitated. The *Telegraph* newspapers turned their ire against Bristol and Durham, who were experimenting with special arrangements for students from weak state schools.[70] *The Times* then unearthed the story that the daughter of the Afro-Caribbean Chairman of the Council on

development of Government policy, which is increasingly concerned with intervening in higher education in order to achieve political objectives. While many of the aims covered in the plan may be laudable in themselves, and indeed are supported by this University, we are very concerned at the overall implications of these developments for the future autonomy of the sector.

'There is an ambiguity running through the document as to whether higher education is part of the public sector (like, for example, the NHS), or whether HEFCE does indeed, as stated in the plan, "recognize that universities and colleges are autonomous institutions and should decide for themselves how best to lead and manage their activities" (p. 2, para. 1). We note for example that the draft plan proposes key performance targets through which the Funding Council can "demonstrate", in measurable terms, our progress towards the aims and objectives [in the plan]. These performance targets are provisional until formally approved by the Secretary of State. In many respects, therefore, the plan seems to imply that higher education is to become an intensively managed part of the public sector.

'This does not reflect the position of this institution, which is an independent self-governing organization, responsible for its own management and development. Whilst Oxford is in receipt of substantial public funding and is keen to account fully for the use of such funds and to demonstrate that they provide an excellent investment, it does not believe that Government and its agencies should assume responsibility for the future strategic direction of this university.' *Oxford University Gazette*, supplement, 4 June 2003.

69. '5.5bn buys single-track universities' and 'OFT warns against price-fixing', *Times Higher Education Supplement*, 7 March 2003.

70. 'Good schools bar to university place', *Daily Telegraph*, 1 March 2003; 'Being clever not always enough for university', *ibid*.

Racial Equality was turned down by Bristol because she had been
to a private school.[71] The independent schools then called for a boycott of Bristol[72] and Bristol appeared to back down.[73] Meanwhile,
appearing before the House of Commons Education Committee,
Secretary Clarke said there had to be targets for working-class students. He pointed out that when Bristol accepted nine per-cent
working-class students and Wolverhampton 48 per cent something
appeared to be wrong. He wanted less emphasis on A levels and
more emphasis on 'a range of other indicators' including SATs[74]
(apparently unaware that SATs are under attack in the United
States for being racially and class biased).[75] HEFCE responded by
taking £265m from teaching funds to reward universities that took
more working-class and lower-achieving students.[76] The *Economist*
pointed out the obvious: 'What caste is to India and race is to
America, class is to Britain' and warned the government against

---

71. 'Young, gifted and black – but not good enough for Bristol University', *Sunday
Telegraph*, 8 March 2003. Although vouched for by the father, Trevor Phillips, it was later
denied by the daughter! See also 'Why class consciousness is rife at Bristol', *Daily Telegraph*,
1 March 2003; 'Inside a university challenged', *Observer*, 9 March 2003.

72. 'Private schools call for boycott of university', *Financial Times*, 5 March 2003.

73. 'Bristol to look at new system of screening applicants', *Financial Times*, 6 March 2003.
The climb-down involved taking academics out of the admissions loop and substituting
American-style admissions recruiters. This was apparently enough to persuade the public
schools to abandon their boycott.

74. 'Varsities told not just to rely on A-levels', *Daily Telegraph*, 6 March 2003. The Secretary
admitted that the long-term solution was better teaching in schools, pointing out that if 11-
year-olds failed to reach level 4 in basic subjects in national tests they had little hope of passing five GCSEs five years later. The NUT, at its conference at Easter 2003, attempted to solve
that problem by voting to abolish the national tests!

75. See also the President of the University of California, Richard C. Atkinson, 'The
California Crucible: Demography, Excellence and Access at the University of California',
Council for Advancement and Support of Education, 2 July 2001, calling for SATs to be abandoned in favour of tests 'that assess mastery of specific academic subject areas rather than aptitude.' That sounded rather like A levels.

76. 'Universities receive extra cash to attract working classes', *The Times*, 7 March 2003.

going down a route about to be abandoned in the USA. At least the flap led Secretary Clarke to overrule his Higher Education Minister, who had called for fixed quotas of poor students to be met by universities.[77] Secretary Clarke was also forced to overrule the overenthusiastic HEFCE plan for targets for working-class students.[78] The Access Regulator was to be told not to set targets, but concentrate on increasing the number of working-class students.[79] Perhaps illogically the Higher Education Minister, Margaret Hodge, announced plans to fine universities which had high drop-out rates.[80] (All US experience is that economically poorer and more academically marginal students have the highest drop-out rates).[81] Mike Tomlinson, former head of OFSTED (the schools' inspection service), was busy developing an examination based on the International Baccalaureate, with apparently a special track for elite universities.[82]

The responses to the White Paper were wonderfully English. A Cambridge don explained why the government was trying to make him a 'partner in fraud'.[83] The new Chancellor of Oxford (EU Commissioner Chris Patten) argued that top up fees of £3,000 were

---

77.   'Affirmative action, negative reaction' and 'Dumb tests', *Economist*, 8 March 2003. Margaret Hodge backed away to favour psychometric tests, 'universities could set psychometric tests says selection row minister', *Evening Standard*, 11 March 2003.

78.   Sir Howard Newby, in establishing a requirement of being within three per cent of target by 2010, announced: 'We are not prepared to see any institution opt out, it is a condition of grant.' Secretary Clarke said that looked too much like quotas. 'Clarke scraps university targets for the poorest', *The Times*, 14 March 2003.

79.   'Access regulator will not set targets', *The Times*, 31 March 2003.

80.   'Universities face fines for drop-outs', *Observer*, 30 March 2003.

81.   See editorial, *Independent on Sunday*, 11 August 2003: 'College is for learning, not a cure for unemployment'.

82.   'Pupils could face tougher exam for elite universities', *The Times*, 31 March 2003.

83.   John Adamson, 'We dons are being asked to destroy what we hold most dear', *Sunday Telegraph*, 9 March 2003.

totally inadequate.[84] Patten went on at his inauguration to attack 'two decades of public parsimony', coupled with 'growing interference'. He added: 'We have put at risk academic standards by falsely perceiving and asserting a tension between them and equality of opportunity. The result has often been, perversely, to curtail the chances of advancement by talented young men and women from poorer backgrounds.'[85] The American psychologist Vice-Chancellor of Brunel University, Steven Schwartz, admitting that 'you cannot make up for schools' deficiencies at university level', announced that his university would establish a boarding school for working–class students on campus.[86] Such enthusiasm led to Professor Schwartz being appointed as advisor to Secretary Clarke on admissions, where he immediately proposed recruiters on the American model and showed that he failed to understand the rationale for the Oxbridge admissions system.[87]

As Easter approached, the government climbed down from its more extreme demands about the Access Regulator. Secretary

---

84.   'Top–up fees of £3,000 not enough, says Patten', *The Times*, 7 March 2003.

85.   'Oxford's new Chancellor promises to challenge funding crisis', *Daily Telegraph*, 26 June 2003.

86.   'University plans boarding school for the working class', *Sunday Telegraph*, 16 March 2003.

87.   'Dons should not choose university students', *Sunday Telegraph*, 13 April 2003. Schwartz had been a professor at Illinois and Texas (both good research universities with indifferent undergraduate programmes) and Vice-Chancellor of Murdoch University in Australia. While admission recruiters are accepted in many American universities, they are rarely trained and not looked on with favour at leading universities. Alan Ryan, 'The message from the US is that there is just about nothing that UK universities can learn from admission practices over here', *Times Higher Education Supplement*, 9 May 2003. The rationale for the Oxbridge admission system is that since fellows are the primary teachers of the undergraduates they admit, and since they remain educationally and morally responsible for them, the tutor should be actively involved in the admissions process. For some Oxford support for the Schwartz position, however, see N. G. McCrum, C. L. Brudin and A. H. Halsey, 'Access: A Better Way', *Oxford Magazine*, fourth week, Trinity Term 2003. Dame Fiona Caldecott, Chair of the Conference of Colleges admitted: 'In the longer term, we are considering a system where applicants apply straight to the university.' 'Ivy clad to Ivy League', *Times Higher Education Supplement*, 30 June 2003.

Clarke admitted that universities' admissions policies were 'generally fair'. OFFA – the Office for Fair Access – (as it was now formally know) would have no power to intervene in admissions policies, but might suggest 'milestones' for raising the numbers of students from 'poorer economic groups'. It seemed that effort and
goals for access would be enough to justify top-up fees.[88]
Universities were relieved; the left thought it was a sell-out.[89] The
independent schools increasingly called for anonymous admissions.[90] Dons at Oxford called for a vote to reject top-up fees –
apparently reflecting an alliance between those who accepted the
view that the poor would suffer and those who wanted to be free of
the yoke of OFFA.[91] It was, in short, not immediately obvious that
there was a dramatic change in what the *Economist* described as 'the
micro-managed and cash strapped [university] system of today'.[92]
Indeed, the to-ings and fro-ings about the Access Regulator remind
one of Milton Friedman's warnings that when one starts tampering
with the market, one has to go on tampering at an exponential rate.
In turn, Secretary Clarke's effort to give freedom to the universities
was reminiscent of the urban myth about the Chinese politburo:
having decided to introduce a market system ('Marxism with
Chinese characteristics') they at once sent a mission to the West to
find out who allocated materials.[93]

88.   Department for Education and Skills, *Widening Participation in Higher Education*, 2003.

89.   'Offtoff huff off', *Economist*, 12 April 2003; 'Universities must show they are open to all',
The Times, 9 April 2003; 'Watchdog to keep powers on university top-up fees', *Financial Times*,
12 April 2003.

90.   'Make college admissions anonymous, say heads', *Evening Standard*, 10 April 2003.

91.   *Oxford University Gazette*, supplement, 3 April 2003.

92.   'Offtoff huff off', *Economist*, 12 April 2003.

93.   Certainly some of those allegedly most in favour of allowing more freedom to the universities also put forward the idea that Russell Group universities should either give up their
undergraduate programmes or only be able to recruit undergraduates locally.

Epilogue

If, indeed, universities do have an element of independence returned to them, they will be fighting against two powerful elements in the English constitution and political process. First, when central government has seized control of some part of society it does not easily abandon that control. Whatever the rhetoric and whichever the party, ever-increasing centralisation has been the order of the day. Second, an intellectual approach to power appears to be alien to the British people. For instance, discussions of civil rights or the powers of a second chamber might be thought to involve an analysis of what constraints, or checks and balances, should be put on parliamentary sovereignty, which has come to mean sovereignty of the House of Commons. Far from accepting this concept, most politicians deny the need for such analysis. Although New Labour consciously gave away part of parliamentary sovereignty with the Human Rights Act, the Home Secretary in the second New Labour administration, David Blunkett, is much given to expressing outrage that the judges are making decisions that ought to be made by the elected representatives in the House of Commons. Similarly, discussions of reform in the House of Lords invariably ignore the fundamental question of how far the second House should fetter the untrammelled claims to sovereignty of the House of Commons. Instead the debate becomes distracted by the question of whether twenty per cent or eighty per cent of the Lords should be elected.

Will this same fate await the suggestion that the universities should have some of their original – at least in the case of the older universities – independence returned to them? While the political centre may think the Clarke Report a successful balancing act, its enemies are legion. The vice-chancellors of most of the old universities and some of the new are reconciled (or attracted) to top-up fees, without which, being realistic about probable future government funding, the decline of universities and the demoralisation of staff are likely to continue; the bulk of academics remain opposed. The Russell Group formally endorsed the Report,[1] with the exception of the Access Regulator.[2] In general, however, the universities' response to the White Paper was their traditional one – whinging.[3] Indeed Secretary Clarke explained his outburst over utopian concepts of the universities as the result of his being upset about the many demands for limitless state funding of higher education: 'What has struck me about the post-White Paper discussions is what I can only describe as a utopianism that says everybody should fund everything at all times to an indefinite level. I do not think that is seriously just or political-

---

1.   In 2003 the Russell Group took the formal step of developing its own staff and organisation. It had grown to a group of some twenty universities, including a few that did not belong there. Its new style was reflected in its demand that the ceiling on fees be raised to £5,000. 'Top universities move to raise ceiling on fees', *Financial Times*, 26-27 July 2003.

2.   'University access debate comes to schools', *Financial Times*, 30 January 2003. In the House of Commons, Secretary Clarke had said the key to access was improving school standards.

3.   Exemplified by the response of Universities UK. See *Universities UK's response to The Future of Higher Education*, April 2003. For a leader urging the universities to get behind top-up fees, see 'Academic Question: Universities must forcefully back up ministers on top-up fees', *The Times*, 27 August 2003. The AUT's contribution was to put down a motion at the Trades Union Congress opposing top-up fees. 'Labour revolt expected over reform', *Financial Times*, 1 September 2003.

ly feasible. So it then raises for me the question of what really is the justification of the State's funding of universities, and I think this argument is worth having.'[4]

At the new universities, the threat of further centralisation of research and the feasibility of ending up as primarily teaching institutions were causes of frustration,[5] as was the fear that weaker universities might go to the wall. At the older universities, the academic politicians are often the remnants of sixties liberals or radicals who thought the government had a non-dischargeable duty to provide funds. Risk-averse by nature, they would have been horrified by any document that proposed change. The NUS, who disapproved of up-front fees but had said they could live with a postgraduate payment, have discovered that they are opposed to any payment and would like full maintenance grants too.[6] No doubt, in time, reformers will discover that the Crawford-Barr repayment scheme for fees is close to a graduate tax and not a hypothecated repayment scheme. The AUT and its allies were appalled at the idea that merit might enter into pay or that different universities should have different missions, not to mention different pay scales;

---

4.   'Dismayed Clarke started debate after "utopian" responses to paper', *Times Higher Education Supplement*, 30 May 2003.

5.   In 1996 the NUS had abandoned demands for universal full grants. In 2003, influenced by the son of then Foreign Secretary Jack Straw, they once more demanded an end to fees and full maintenance grants irrespective of parental wealth, all to be paid out of more progressive taxation. 'NUS left forces U-turn on grants', *Times Higher Education Supplement*, 4 April 2003.

6.   The AUT deplored the polarisation of teaching and research; NATFHE deplored 'research selectivity' and warned, 'We are going back towards the world of polytechnics.' '5.5bn buys single-track universities', *Times Higher Education Supplement*, 7 March 2003. The recommendation merely underlined the existing situation. For 2002/3, the HEFCE grant to Cambridge was £53m for teaching and £136m for research; for Wolverhampton, £43m for teaching and £590,000 for research. See also David R. Stiles, 'Higher Education Funding Council (HEFC) Methods in the 1990s: National and Regional Developments and Policy Implications', *Public Administration*, vol. 80, (2002) p. 711.

and they soon had an opportunity to panic when Imperial College announced a local salary scale.[7]

It is not the NUS, AUT or the *Economist* who will count, however, but the politicians. Already, Paul Farrelly, the organiser of the Early Day Motion, has nearly 200 Labour and Liberal Democrat signers who will oppose any effort to implement the Clarke plan in this Parliament. The relative success of the war in Iraq probably means that Tony Blair will remain leader of the Labour Party for a period, although he could be undercut by revelations about the manipulation of intelligence documents and advisers and the inability to stabilise Iraq after the fighting finished.[8] Blair's position, however, was ironic, in that, after the Iraq War, he was more popular in the country (and in the United States) than in the party. Gordon Brown's apparent loyalty during the fighting means that he will probably succeed Blair, although his limited appeal to Middle England could halt the collapse of the Conservative Party. If Blair, however, were to be replaced by Brown relatively soon,[9] the White Paper may well be dead; if David Blunkett becomes leader, it probably is. If Charles Clarke is the new leader,[10] then the White Paper could be

7.   The Rector of Imperial, Sir Richard Sykes, had already arbitrarily ignored the lower rungs of the national scale to pay a basic beginning salary of £28,000. He now planned to move Imperial away from the national salary scale. A source in the AUT said: 'This is tough for the AUT. Its members at Imperial will get better pay from this local arrangement, as will AUT members in other top universities if they follow suit, but the union will not want to concede the fundamental principle of national bargaining.' 'National pay under threat', *Times Higher Education Supplement*, 30 May 2003.

8.   For an analysis of Blair's position in the light of the Hutton Inquiry, see 'In the dock', *Economist*, 30 August 2003.

9.   Charles Clarke continued to attempt to compromise with signers of the Early Day Motion, for instance, by floating the idea of an extension of maintenance grants. 'Clarke signals compromise in top-up fees row', *Daily Telegraph*, 17 May 2003.

10.   On this possibility, see 'Now who's knocking louder on Tony's door', *Observer*, 26 January 2003. His star rather faded after the fiasco of funding in primary and secondary schools. Bagehot, 'Charles Clarke fails the test', *Economist*, 7 June 2003. Conspiracy theorists argued that the Chancellor had orchestrated the crisis to undermine a potential competitor to succeed Blair.

fully implemented. Certainly the intention of the government in the summer of 2003 was to stand firm, and the appointment of Alan Johnson[11] – a tough trade unionist with no university background – in place of Margaret Hodge as Higher Education Minister suggested an intention to stay with top-up fees.[12] In the short run the Chancellor's lukewarm support for foundation hospitals[13] suggests that the whips may have difficulty pushing through legislation to implement the White Paper in this session, particularly in view of the Conservative and Liberal Democrat positions.[14] At the same time the Fifth Report of the Select Committee on Education, in many ways a tougher version of the White Paper, could provide support for the government. Moreover, the truce hinted at between Brown and Blair during the summer recess, allegedly allowing Brown to become Prime Minister two years into the next Parliament, may make the Brownites more willing to be flexible on top-up fees.[15]

The Conservatives' position, with weak leadership, was unpredictable. There was a hope they might adopt the views of Robert Jackson and throw a lifeline to Charles Clarke. Jackson, the former Higher Education Minister, pointed out that the universities had 'only very recently been nationalised – with the usual deplorable

---

11. 'Johnson faces cool reception', *Times Higher Education Supplement*, 20 June 2003. His full title is the Minister for Lifelong Learning, Further and Higher Education. He is a vigorous supporter of the White Paper.

12. 'Government giving no ground on top-up fees as rebellion grows', *Times Higher Education Supplement*, 27 June 2003.

13. For the argument that the present Blair–Brown duopoly will survive, see Bagehot, 'The ties that do bind', *Economist*, 24 May 2003.

14. The bill is now drafted, together with various possible amendments designed to placate the dissidents.

15. 'Blair and Brown agree on regime change at No. 10', *The Times*, 8 August 2003; 'The heat has gone out of Downing Street rivalry', *ibid*. That was certainly not obvious at the Labour Party Conference in the autumn of 2003

consequences – it would be perverse for Conservatives to oppose a measure of denationalisation from a Labour government'. There was even a hope that the party would take seriously the warning from former Conservative Education Secretary, Kenneth Baker, that 'when great institutions decline, they do not decline precipitously: there is no precipice. They simply decline very slowly. Higher education is now heading down that slope ...'.[16] The party, however, chose to endorse the tactical view of Ken Clarke, to gain the votes of Middle England and watch the universities sink. In May 2003 they announced the cynical policy of abandoning a fifty per cent goal and getting rid of 'Mickey Mouse courses' (did this mean golf management at Birmingham, military science at Sandhurst, or sociology at Plymouth?). By using the money 'saved' (clearly no one had done the costing) they would abolish all fees (since the money for a fifty per cent goal had never been allocated, the plan was misleading from an economic point of view). The policy was decided upon over a 'bonding weekend' of Tory MPs in Buckinghamshire. It was based on the result of a YouGov poll (IDS's favourite pollster since it was the only one showing the Conservatives in the lead), showing that this policy would buy the party more votes than any other policy.[17] Getting rid of the Access Regulator was also popular. The *volte-face* strengthened the hand of Labour's left, and it will ensure the continuing demise of the

---

16. Jackson and Baker went to Iain Duncan Smith to urge him to support the White Paper. They found that Smith had difficulty grasping the issues. Influenced by his PR and advertising gurus, Smith opted to go with the YouGov poll. He did not even bother to inform Sir Robert Balchin, Chair of the Conservative Education Commission or the hard-working Baroness Blatch, Conservative spokesperson on education in the Lords.

17. Conservative Central Office, *Duncan Smith: A fair deal for everyone*, 13 May 2003. See also 'Tories vow to abolish university tuition fees', *Financial Times*, 13 May 2003; *Financial Times* Martin Wolf, 'A morally bankrupt education policy', *ibid.*, 26 May 2003. For support for the Conservative position, see Jenny McCartney, 'Free universities for a select few: now that's a novel idea', *Sunday Telegraph*, 18 May 2003.

8888ЙЙЙ

English universities,[18] although it might just force the leading universities to declare independence – as they still legally may – and charge real fees, and thereby require Middle England to pay rather more than the £3,000 top-up fee.

The new policy must have been faintly embarrassing for the Conservative leadership. Damian Green, the shadow Education Secretary, had said he saw nothing wrong with variable fees. As to the existing Blunkett top-up fees, only a third of students paid them because they were means tested. The YouGov plan was therefore geared to the wealthiest voters. With respect to abandoning the future £3,000 fee, the income tax to fund the 'free' higher education would come primarily from the less wealthy taxpayers so that the changes would make the poorest tenth of households 1.5 per cent worse off and the top tenth 0.4 per cent better off.[19] When in June 2003 the Conservatives introduced a motion in the House of Commons supporting, apparently, the views of the National Union of Students on fees, the weakness of the Conservative arguments became clear. They admitted that there would be fewer places at universities,[20] but cited in their support two Tory enemies – the National Union of Teachers and the Association of Teachers and Lecturers. During the debate, it became painfully obvious that the Conservative proposals had not been costed, were shamelessly slanted to the wealthy and would push some universities into bankruptcy. As the Vice-Chancellor of the

---

18. 'How nice, briefly, to be a Tory', *Economist*, 24 May 2003: 'breathtaking cynicism'. The one thing that might help with the 173 signers of the 'Early Day' Motion is that virtually all universities appeared set to charge £3,000 by way of top-up fees, thereby muting the fears of a two-tier system. Ironically, Margaret Hodge was threatening new universities which charged £3000 without justification. 'Hodge: We will control market', *Times Higher Education Supplement*, 23 May 2003.

19. Institute of Fiscal Studies, *Study Now, Pay Later or HE for Free*, 2003.

20. E.g. Damian Green, *Parliamentary Debates*, H. of C., vol. 408, col. 1059 (25 June 2003). Charles Clarke estimated up to 150,000 fewer, *ibid*, col. 1071.

independent University of Buckingham put it: 'Why are the Tories now sinking into louche populism?' It was perhaps significant that only a handful of Tory MPs attended the debate.

Perhaps the party with the greater ability to do damage is the Liberal Democrats, increasingly seen as the second most important party. Contaminated by their parochial leaders north of the border in Scotland, where they are in government with Labour, they argue nationally against all fees and for larger maintenance grants. This wins them a wide range of support from Middle England[21] and also attracts the left wing of Labour voters.[22] The Liberal Democrats' proposals for requiring all those who wish to receive a university maintenance grant first to spend two years at a further education college has received less publicity; it would not be popular in middle England. The fact that their proposals will do nothing to give any freedom or diversity to universities and that the additional taxation they propose will probably be hijacked on its way to the universities, by the demands of the NHS and schools, is irrelevant.

The Liberal Democrats have, however, pushed on with their policies, and produced a much more courageous Commons motion than the Conservatives had managed, calling for an end to all fees.[23] They were especially proud of what they had wrought in Scotland – a graduate tax that went, not to the universities, but to an endowment that provided maintenance grants.[24] The motion was defeated, backbench Labour MPs electing 'to fight another day'.[25]

21. For more of this, see 'Family shaken by prospect of a bill for £100,000', *The Times*, 23 January 2003; 'More tiers for students in Clarke shake-up', *Daily Telegraph*, 23 January 2003.

22. E.g. Phil Willis, Liberal Democrat education spokesman, attacking Clarke's proposals as establishing a two-tier system. 'University shake-up clears the way for fees.' *Financial Times*, 23 January 2003.

23. *Parl. Deb.*, House of Commons, vol. 407, col. 724 (23 June 2003)

24. See per Peter Duncan, *ibid*, col. 756.

25. 'Labour top-up fee opponents elect to fight another day', *The Times*, 24 June 2003.

One might have thought that the Conservative and Liberal Democrat debates, coming after the Clarke White Paper, might be enough excitement for one session. It was not to be. Of course there were the usual political games. The *Scotsman* saw the replacement of Blair by Brown as imminent.[26] The unions and Labour's backbenchers had so watered down the foundation hospital proposals – closely linked to top-up fees – that they will scarcely be distinguishable from their predecessors and the National Health Service is likely to continue to limp into decline. The interim Report from Richard Lambert castigated the universities – and particularly Oxford and Cambridge – for their lack of entrepreneurial ethos and slow involvement with knowledge transfer.[27] Cambridge's management was particularly bad and the refusal to give the new Vice-Chancellor executive powers evidence of a 'closed and inward looking' organisation. Oxford came off rather better, but it too needed a 'sharp business approach'; and the government might have to intervene if the two universities did not reform their governance, which appeared to mean that the college system should be quietly put out of its misery.[28] Overall, the message was, as one might expect from the former editor of the *Financial Times*, a steely economic one: there should be regional hubs for technology transfer and credit in the RAEs for forming partnerships with industry.[29] There

---

26. 'Blair's grip on power slippery: Brown's allies prepare for Chancellor to seize control', *Scotsman*, 14 July 2003.

27. The Treasury, *Lambert Review of Business–University Collaboration: Summary of Consultation Responses and Emerging Issues*, July 2003. 'Oxbridge told: shape up or lose freedom: Dithering dons risk world-class status, says Treasury adviser', *The Times*, 15 July 2003. See also 'Academics and executives face a deep divide', *Financial Times*, 29 July 2003.

28. It has been speculated that Oxford and Cambridge will be given one last chance to reform before the government steps in to ensure greater executive powers in the centre with more outsiders involved. Professor Gillian Evans, who had helped sabotage the Cambridge reforms, announced: 'We are not intimidated by the threat of outside action. We are extremely influential people.' 'Academics resist a higher degree of interference', *Financial Times*, 26-27 July 2003.

29. 'Oxford and Cambridge "need sharp business approach"', *Financial Times*, 15 July 2003.

appeared to be support for further centralisation of research, stream-lining and some reduction of accountability (currently being looked at by the VandeLinde review group) and better ways of having industry influence the skills and substance of higher education. In short, the interim Report reflected the Treasury's *dirigiste* approach to higher education, its obsession with the link between industry and universities, and its belief that universities have been badly run. (The irony is that the Treasury's forays into educational administration have been a disaster: e.g. lifelong learning accounts and the University of Industry.)

What perhaps was most startling, however, was the Report on Higher Education of the Select Committee on Education and Skills.[30] The Chairman, Barry Sheerman, had, over time, spoken intelligently about the 'long-term future of higher education', and had generally welcomed the Clarke White Paper. Yet building on the earlier work of the Committee, the MPs – seven Labour, three Conservative and one Liberal Democrat – produced a unanimous Report (with the Liberal Democrats offering the usual objection to fees and demanding higher taxation). It was a Report which may prove to be a critical statement about the long-term future of higher education in England.

The Report was interesting in that it criticised the White Paper for being relatively short-termist, and for failing to emphasise the role of universities in the 'successful development of the potential of individuals ... [Universities] are at the very heart of the maintenance of an intellectually vigorous and civilised society'. The Report admitted that universities played an important part in economic success, but the Report tried to put education ahead of the economy as the primary purpose of universities. Compared with the White Paper, the Report emphasised the popularity of English universities with overseas stu-

---

30. Select Committee on Education and Skills, *Fifth Report*, HMSO, 10 July 2003.

dents.[31] With the cost to the Exchequer of universities reaching some £10 billion by 2006, the Committee shared the White Paper's view that the costs should be shared between the student, the government and the employer. The Committee, however, was prepared to push this last source more dramatically than Secretary Clarke. It proposed a tax for firms that did not undertake significant research and development, to be used as a research fund for universities.[32]

Perhaps surprisingly the Report called for greater independence and diversity for universities. The top-up fee could be up to £5,000, not £3,000, if it were intended to provide a serious market. Access should be left to HEFCE and the Office of Fair Access abandoned. The idea that there be an access premium, skimmed off the block grant, caused concern, as did any arbitrary goal for numbers in higher education.[33] There was especial concern that expansion might be too linked to the establishment of foundation degrees. Indeed, the Committee vigorously insisted that it was the absence of maintenance grants, not fees, that deterred the poor from attending universities. Thus the Committee recommended that loans ceased to be subsidised, so that maintenance grants of up to £5,000 p.a. might be paid to those of poorer backgrounds out of the money saved.[34] This would be in addition to waiving fees for the poor.

---

31.   True. But whereas UK universities have been more successful than continental universities in attracting overseas students, American universities have become relatively far more popular with foreign students than UK universities over the last twenty-five years. This trend is likely to continue as countries such as Singapore and Hong Kong revise their educational systems along American rather than British lines. Similarly, the well-publicised doubts about A levels will undermine the tradition of taking those exams in Commonwealth countries.

32.   *Report on Higher Education*, para. 188.

33.   With more than ninety per cent of those with two A levels going to university, the Committee felt some of the goals unrealistic. Besides which, natural growth will take care of the matter. By 2010 it is estimated that forty-six per cent of all students will have two or more A levels. *Ibid*, para. 106.

34.   *Ibid*, para. 207.

The other things that concerned the Committee included the relationship of teaching and research, particularly with respect to the concept that there might be research-free universities. It was the age-old battle of the link between teaching and research, with the Committee siding with the traditional academic arguments.[35] All universities should be free to develop their own trajectories and, while it was inevitable that much of research would be concentrated in the international universities, there was a strong case for research funds to be distributed more broadly, with some consideration of regional developments. Secretary Clarke was criticised for channelling research funds to fewer institutions even before the Roberts Report had been discussed, yet alone agreed; and a case was made for restoring funding to departments with RAE 4s.[36]

The Committee was especially concerned about the 'woefully low' salaries in academic life, pointing out that the six per cent increase in funding for each of the next three years was geared heavily to research and there would be no funds for real increases in salaries.[37] Other shibboleths were knocked down. As part of the scepticism about universities' primary responsibility to the economy, the Committee poured cold water on knowledge exchanges.[38] As the Report concluded: 'A significant conclusion of the White Paper is that the Government sees universities and colleges principally as economic agents; there is very little in the document about intellectual or cultural life in higher education, or the broader development of the individual.'[39] Coupled with

---

35.   *Ibid*, para. 52.

36.   *Ibid*, paras. 45–52. And see 'We believe … that the flame of research endeavour should be kept alive in all universities, and that each region of the UK should have within it a focus for the highest quality, internationally competitive research'. Summary, *ibid*.

37.   The Committee suggested that rather than spending money on centres of teaching excellence, the money should go to improve salaries. *Ibid*, paras. 83–5.

38.   *Ibid*, para. 66.

39.   *Ibid*, para. 213.

an injunction to the government not 'to micro-manage what universities do', the Report gained the support of both of all the Labour members (including two who had signed the Early Day Motion) and of all three Conservatives (including Robert Jackson). It was a remarkable achievement by Chairman Sheerman.

While the *Times Higher Education Supplement* was probably wrong to say that the Committee 'savaged the White Paper',[40] in many ways the Select Committee Report was better argued, looked more to the future, and was better balanced than the White Paper. The immediate hope was that the Report might discourage Labour backbenchers from sabotaging top-up fees; but Charles Clarke was not instantly about to accept the Committee's advice. With the Chancellor breathing down his neck, he defended the £3,000 cap for top-up fees, OFFA, the centralisation of research and foundation degrees, as well as arguing that the end of the interest subsidy would hurt the poor. The government provided both a response to the Select Committee and other responses to the White Paper during the summer and provided a House of Commons debate in September. The formal response was, in the words of the *Financial Times*, 'uncompromising'. Secretary Clarke was not about to make changes, except that he attempted to rechristen top-up fees as an 'individualised graduate tax'.[41] The limit for fees was to be £3,000, the Access Regulator remained and while the government might consider remitting fees to poorer students, there was no possibility of serious maintenance grants. Concentration of research was reaffirmed and

---

40. Sheerman said: 'The White Paper marks a unique moment in the history of higher education and if this opportunity is missed, then we are going to regret it for a very long time.' 'MPs savage White Paper proposals', *Times Higher Education Supplement*, 11 July 2003.

41. 'Graduate tax is new spin on top-up fee', *The Times*, 26 August 2003; 'Ministers set for new push over tuition fees', *Financial Times*, 26 August 2003.

there was certainly no intention of funding departments that had scored 4 in the RAEs. Secretary Clarke also reaffirmed that 'expansion will be based around economic trends and demands'. There was apparently to be no truck with classical notions of a broader education.[42] As Barry Sheerman put it: 'It's all honeyed words and phrases.'[43] An outsider might suggest it sounded as if the Committee was being quietly told to mind its own business.

With Parliament in recess, the government appeared to be willing to go down to the wire on the White Paper solutions. Perhaps they will be helped by the Education Committee's Report; or perhaps the latter Report could take on a life of its own. The Conservatives maintained their policy of 'opportunism over integrity' as the new Higher Education Minister put it. No alternative solution which might help save the quality of universities was advanced in the febrile atmosphere in which English politics is played out. Parents, students and staff overwhelmingly did not want fees. Better to have the universities decline. Jimmy the Greek would not give decent odds on the Clarke plan, let alone the Select Committee's Report, surviving, which is a pity.[44] Unlike the Dearing Report, the Clarke White Paper has vision – and is written in English.[45] The Sheerman Report actually thought about the long-term future of higher education. Those attributes alone will be enough to frighten off most of the punters.

42.   Department for Education and Skills, *Government response to Select Committee and White Paper on the future of Higher Education*, press release, 28 July 2003.

43.   'Universities threatened with tuition charge fines', *Financial Times*, 29 July 2003.

44.   For a robust explanation of how thinking about universities will have to change, see John Clare and Rachel Sylvester, 'Students may have to work through college and live at home, says Clarke', *Daily Telegraph*, 25 January 2003. E.g. 'The finishing school aspects of university shouldn't be a central part of university life, they're not for government funding.' See also 'Tuition fee plans put paid to dreams of a gap year', *Financial Times*, 25–26 January 2003.

45.   Unlike the Dearing Report, which was effectively written by the Department for Education, HEFCE was responsible for much of the White Paper.

Afterword

As Christmas 2003 approaches and the page proof goes to the printer to be turned into books, remarkably little has changed.

What is clearer than ever is the remarkable courage of Tony Blair's and Charles Clarke's attempt to offer universities greater academic and financial freedom; indeed, to begin to solve their financial crisis. It was an effort to restore independence to a sector that had over the last two decades become remarkably subject to central control. The Blair–Clarke project was the first effort in recent years to put universities and their needs and quality ahead of the demands of students and parents that everything should be 'free'. At last universities might see their way out of years of underfunding. The success of this effort was, however, increasingly in doubt.

Indeed, New Labour 'project' as a whole was in doubt. Tony Blair's grip on the party in the Commons appeared to be unravelling. In the Lords, Labour seemed to be losing control of government business. The policy of foundation hospitals just squeaked through; the success of top-up fees looked more dubious. The whips threatened; Blair and Clarke made concession after concession, but the prognosis remained gloomy. It was all part of the collateral damage of the war in Iraq.

The biggest danger was the Labour backbenchers who insisted that they could not live with a two-tier system of universities. In a healthy higher education system, there should be as many tiers as there are universities. What Old Labour seemed to want was that unless Oxford was doing what Thames Valley was doing, neither should be well funded. Or, more romantically, that Thames Valley should be funded at a level that enabled it to do what Oxford did. The logic of this argument was that it was more important to dumb down universities than to fund serious international universities.

The Liberal Democrats also saw no sense in independent universities. In the Commons, they sought to cash in on the student vote and student demands – inevitably short-term interests. In the Lords, Baroness Williams seemed anxious to finish off the academic universities, as she had the academic high schools thirty years earlier.

It was perhaps the Conservatives, however, who won the prize for cynically undermining what some saw as the best last chance of rescuing the universities. Having ditched the hapless Iain Duncan Smith, the Tories under Michael Howard embraced his unprincipled approach to higher education with enthusiasm. Not only were affluent parents to be 'given' the means-tested fees they previously had to pay, they were promised no top-up fees. Coupled with the continuing commitment to dramatically lower taxation, the future of the English universities could be bleak if the Conservatives were ever returned.

For the old academic universities undergraduate programmes were loss leaders. The temptation to do an LSE and fill such programmes with affluent students from abroad would be difficult to resist. Further decline in undergraduate education would be inevitable, while self-financing graduate programmes would grow. A few universities might consider the option of declaring independence. If the government declared that such a step would lead to ineligibility for research grants, the threat would evaporate. Even in the absence of such a threat, the innate caution of academic staff would make it unlikely that university leaders would have the support to carry through such a significant privatisation. Loss of the top-up-fee solution would be close to a disaster.

4 December 2003

Index

dislike of universities 38

free-market approach to universities 58

has her honorary Oxford degree publicly rejected by dons 49

increases goals for higher education 40

Keith Joseph's loyalty to 50

lack of time for teachers or teaching unions 55

means-testing on university maintenance grants 51

renowned in America as guru of freedom and the market 45

saves the Open University 38

Thatcherism in education 63

toppled by Tory rebels 62

tries to have Sir William Pile sacked 38

views on student protests during 1960s 38-39

withdraws support for Keith Joseph's proposal for lowering the threshold for grants 51

Times 85, 150, 153, 163

Times Higher Education Supplement xvii, 138, 180

Tomlinson, Mike 165

Top-up fees 76, 92, 104, 115, 122, 124, 129, 131-132, 142, 147-148, 150, 169, 172, 178, 180

Tony Blair becomes convert to 126

Tony Blair holds secret meeting with Vice-Chancellors who support 127

180 back-bench MPs sign motion opposing 127

Top-Up Loans for Students (1988) 61

Tower Hamlets College of Further Education xii-xiii

Trade Union Congress xiv

Treasury xv, 16, 63, 87, 94-95, 101, 133, 149

refuses to increase size of university fees during 1970s 46

University of Industry (see University of Industry)

Trinity College, Oxford 26

Trow, Martin vii

Ulster, University of xvi, 121

United States of America ix, 57, 65-66, 85, 94, 101-103, 111-112, 120-122, 136, 141-142, 148, 164-165, 171

brain drain to 54

Britain attempts to emulate American High Schools 28

credit system 158

GI Bill introduced in colleges and universities post WWII 14

Ivy League institutions 100-101, 113, 121, 136, 152

modular system in 53

University Funding Council (UFC) 68, 88

replaces UGC 58-59

University Grants Committee (UGC) 12, 19, 22, 25-26, 33, 40, 49, 63, 68, 106, 125, 162

abolished by Kenneth Baker and replaced with UFC 58-59

agrees to distribute research funds more selectively 57

attempts to become planning agency 47

Committee on Grants to University Colleges (1889) 12

golden period of 31

government cuts basic grants 42

government reviews constitutional position of 56

state's need for the 'outline of a central strategy' 46

Universities Branch 26

Universities UK (see also the Committee of Vice Chancellors and Principals)